Building Applications on Mesos

David Greenberg

Beijing · Boston · Farnham · Sebastopol · Tokyo

Building Applications on Mesos

by David Greenberg

Copyright © 2016 David Greenberg. All rights reserved.

Printed in the United States of America.

Published by O'Reilly Media, Inc., 1005 Gravenstein Highway North, Sebastopol, CA 95472.

O'Reilly books may be purchased for educational, business, or sales promotional use. Online editions are also available for most titles (*http://safaribooksonline.com*). For more information, contact our corporate/institutional sales department: 800-998-9938 or *corporate@oreilly.com*.

Editors: Rachel Roumeliotis and Brian Foster	**Indexer:** Wendy Catalano
Production Editor: Nicholas Adams	**Interior Designer:** David Futato
Copyeditor: Rachel Head	**Cover Designer:** Randy Comer
Proofreader: James Fraleigh	**Illustrator:** Rebecca Demarest

December 2015:   First Edition

Revision History for the First Edition

2015-12-04:   First Release

See *http://oreilly.com/catalog/errata.csp?isbn=9781491926529* for release details.

978-1-491-92652-9

[LSI]

Table of Contents

Preface

Conventions Used in This Book

The following typographical conventions are used in this book:

Italic

> Indicates new terms, URLs, email addresses, filenames, and file extensions.

`Constant width`

> Used for program listings, as well as within paragraphs to refer to program elements such as variable or function names, databases, data types, environment variables, statements, and keywords.

`Constant width italic`

> Shows text that should be replaced with user-supplied values or by values determined by context.

This element signifies a tip or suggestion.

This element signifies a general note.

This element indicates a warning or caution.

Safari® Books Online

Safari Books Online is an on-demand digital library that delivers expert content in both book and video form from the world's leading authors in technology and business.

Technology professionals, software developers, web designers, and business and creative professionals use Safari Books Online as their primary resource for research, problem solving, learning, and certification training.

Safari Books Online offers a range of plans and pricing for enterprise, government, education, and individuals.

Members have access to thousands of books, training videos, and prepublication manuscripts in one fully searchable database from publishers like O'Reilly Media, Prentice Hall Professional, Addison-Wesley Professional, Microsoft Press, Sams, Que, Peachpit Press, Focal Press, Cisco Press, John Wiley & Sons, Syngress, Morgan Kaufmann, IBM Redbooks, Packt, Adobe Press, FT Press, Apress, Manning, New Riders, McGraw-Hill, Jones & Bartlett, Course Technology, and hundreds more. For more information about Safari Books Online, please visit us online.

How to Contact Us

Please address comments and questions concerning this book to the publisher:

O'Reilly Media, Inc.
1005 Gravenstein Highway North
Sebastopol, CA 95472
800-998-9938 (in the United States or Canada)
707-829-0515 (international or local)
707-829-0104 (fax)

We have a web page for this book, where we list errata, examples, and any additional information. You can access this page at *http://bit.ly/building-applications-on-mesos*.

To comment or ask technical questions about this book, send email to *bookquestions@oreilly.com*.

For more information about our books, courses, conferences, and news, see our website at *http://www.oreilly.com*.

Find us on Facebook: *http://facebook.com/oreilly*

Follow us on Twitter: *http://twitter.com/oreillymedia*

Watch us on YouTube: *http://www.youtube.com/oreillymedia*

Acknowledgments

This book took a huge amount of work, and it wouldn't have been possible without the help and support of many people.

First, I'd like to thank Brian Foster and the team at O'Reilly. They did so much to make this book a reality.

I'd also like to thank Two Sigma, my employer, for giving me the time and support to write this book.

The quality of the book was improved immeasurably thanks to the feedback and reviews I received from Matt Adereth, Adam Bordelon, Niklas Nielsen, and David Palaitis.

Finally, I'd like to thank my wife, Aysylu Greenberg, for her love and support throughout the writing process.

CHAPTER 1

Introduction to Mesos

Let's take a trip back in time, to the year 1957. Computers that use transistors are starting to proliferate across universities and research laboratories. There is a problem, though—only one person can use a computer at a time. So, we have paper sign-up sheets so that we can reserve time slots on the machines. Since computers are so much more powerful than pencil and paper, they are in high demand. At the same time, since the computers are so expensive, if people don't use their whole reservations, then thousands of dollars of compute-time could be wasted! Luckily, the idea of operating systems already existed, more or less, at the time. A brilliant man named John McCarthy, who also invented LISP (*http://bit.ly/lispwiki*), had a great idea—what if all the users could submit their jobs to the computer, and the computer would automatically share its CPU resources among the many different jobs?

Jobs Became Programs

What we now call applications or programs used to be called jobs. We still can see this terminology in our shells, where, once we've backgrounded a process, we use the `jobs` command to inspect all the programs we've launched in the shell.

Once a single machine could be shared between jobs, we didn't need humans to supervise the sign-up sheets—now, everyone could use the machine, and share it more easily, since the machine could enforce quotas, priorities, and even egalitarian fairness (if so desired).

Fast-forward to 2010: with the falling costs of networked data transmission and storage, it's now possible to store every bit of information you can collect. To process all this data, you probably need to use Storm (a distributed real-time data processing system) and Hadoop. So, you get a whole mess of machines: a few for the Hadoop

JobTracker and Storm Nimbus (each with its own painstakingly crafted configuration), a few more for the HDFS NameNode and Secondary NameNode, 15 more that you'll install Hadoop TaskTrackers and HDFS DataNodes on, and 10 more that you use to run Storm Supervisors. At this point, you've managed to purchase 30 machines. However, if you decide that instead you'd like to use five of your Hadoop machines as Storm workers, you're in for painful task, because you now need to completely reprovision the Hadoop machines as Storm machines—a process that, as many practitioners can vouch, is not as easy as we'd wish.

It's 2011: the Berkeley AMP lab is in full swing. This is the group that today has brought us Spark, Tachyon, and many other distributed, scalable systems. One of the projects in the lab is called Mesos: it wants to be a platform for sharing your computer cluster between many disparate applications, such as Hadoop and MPI. In the Mesos paper,[1] the authors show promising results in sharing a single cluster of commodity computer hardware between many different applications, including MPI and Hadoop. This effectively solves the reprovisioning problem in clusters. Of course, companies like Google and Yahoo! are interested in the AMP lab, because they're working on similar problems. The team at Twitter take it a step further: they realize that Mesos solves a critical problem with which they've been struggling—how to efficiently wrangle the massive number of machines in their data centers—so, they manage to hire the lead author of the paper and architect of Mesos, PhD candidate Ben Hindman, so that he can tackle this problem at Twitter. Over the next several years, Mesos grows from being a simple research project into the core infrastructure that powers tens of thousands of servers at Twitter and many other companies.

So now that you know a little about Mesos (in the historical sense and context), you probably want to know what Mesos *is* (in the technical sense). Mesos is a system that allows you to harness all of the different machines in your computer cluster or data center and treat them as a single logical entity. With Mesos, the problem of having fixed sets of machines assigned to applications is no longer an issue. Instead, you can easily change which software is running on which machines, or even abdicate the responsibility of choosing which software runs on which machines to Mesos and allow it to make that decision for you, freeing up your time and mind to work on other (more interesting and more important) problems. For instance, in my company, Mesos allowed us to rapidly experiment with new distributed systems, such as Spark and Storm.

---

1 Although most people think of the NSDI 2011 paper "Mesos: A Platform for Fine-Grained Resource Sharing in the Data Center," by Ben Hindman, Andy Konwinski, Matei Zaharia, et al., originally Mesos was published as Nexus in "Nexus: A Common Substrate for Cluster Computing" by the same authors in 2009.

How to Use Mesos

In the simplest sense, Mesos is an orchestration platform for managing CPU, memory, and other resources across a cluster. Mesos uses containerization technology, such as Docker and Linux Containers (LXC), to accomplish this. However, Mesos provides much more than that—it provides real-time APIs for interacting with and developing for the cluster.

Many people wonder where Mesos sits in their stack. Is it part of their deployment infrastructure? Should their infrastructure team manage it? Or is Mesos an application development platform, like Heroku? Maybe Mesos should really belong to an application team… The answer to these questions is not straightforward, because Mesos provides functionality that crosses between Infrastructure as a Service (IaaS) and Platform as a Service (PaaS), in order to achieve greater efficiencies for your system. On the one hand, Mesos is infrastructure: it is the platform on which we deploy Hadoop and Storm and all the other PaaS goodies that we require for business. On the other hand, suppose that we're trying to develop an application that can process large-scale computations, similar to Hadoop or Spark. In that case, Mesos becomes the platform that we are building on. Suddenly, rather than treating it as a black box, we're very much concerned with its APIs and how to develop for it.

In practice, it's best to think of Mesos as serving a different purpose altogether. It allows you to stop focusing on individual machines, whether for developing your applications or for deploying them. Instead, it allows you to treat your cluster as a single, large group of resources. Mesos increases your agility for testing and deploying new distributed systems, as well as providing the platform to deploy in-house applications more quickly and efficiently than if you needed to involve your developer operations (DevOps) organization in those processes. For small projects, Mesos subsumes the many different systems that one might otherwise need to deal with— deployment tools like Ansible, Chef, and Puppet can now be relegated to basic roles in which they bootstrap Mesos. Mesos is the ultimate DevOps tool which thoroughly blurs the lines between the APIs the application runs against and the deployment of the application is a part of: Twitter has just three operators managing its tens-of-thousands-of-node Mesos clusters.

Let's now take a look at how Mesos fills two different roles: deployment system and execution platforms.

Mesos as a Deployment System

One way that you can think about Mesos is as a smart deployment system. First, let's look at a typical deployment system today, like Ansible (*http://www.ansible.com/*) or Chef (*https://www.chef.io/chef/*). To use these tools, you write lists of tasks that should be performed on the various machines in your cluster. Tasks can modify files, install

programs, and interact with supervision systems (like Supervisor (*http://supervi
sord.org/*) and SystemD (*http://www.freedesktop.org/wiki/Software/systemd/*)). Groups
of tasks can be combined to describe a "role" or "recipe," which represents a higher-
level concept, like setting up a database or web server. Finally, these groups of tasks
are applied to an "inventory," or set of hosts, which then configures them according to
the specification.

These tools are wildly more useful than the Bash, Perl, and SSH mashups of old; however, they suffer from fundamental limitations. On the one hand, they allow for configuration to be written in a structured, understandable form. They enable the use of
best practices from software development—source control, encapsulation, and code
reuse through libraries and plug-ins—to extend to system administration. On the
other hand, they are fundamentally designed to make a fleet of machines conform to
a static configuration. This is intentional: once you've run your Ansible or Puppet
configuration, you want the cluster to be in the same, known consistent state. If, however, you want your cluster to dynamically reallocate resources or shift configurations
depending on various external factors, such as the current load, these tools can't help
you.

In this sense, it can be useful to think of Mesos as a deployment system. Distributed
applications can be made into Mesos frameworks for use on a Mesos cluster. Rather
than forcing you to use a static configuration description, each framework is essentially a role or recipe: the framework contains all the logic needed to install, start,
monitor, and use a given application. Many frameworks are themselves platforms;
when many applications follow the same general deployment pattern (like web
servers), then a single framework can manage them all (like Marathon, a Mesos
framework for stateless services). The power of Mesos is that since the framework is a
live, running program, it can make decisions on the fly, reacting to changing workloads and cluster conditions. For instance, a framework could observe how many
resources seem to be available, and change its execution strategy to better perform
given the current cluster conditions. Because the deployment system runs constantly,
it can notice and adapt to failures in real time, automatically starting up new servers
as previous ones fail. Mesos frameworks are strictly more powerful than static
descriptions used by more traditional deployment systems.

Thus, you can think of Mesos as supplanting much of the functionality that Ansible
or Chef previously provided. You'll still need a traditional configuration manager to
bootstrap the Mesos cluster; however, Mesos provides a more powerful platform for
hosting applications: frameworks can automatically and dynamically adapt to failing
machines and changing workloads, giving operators greater peace of mind and time
to work on new initiatives.

Mesos as an Execution Platform

Another way to think of Mesos is as a platform for hosting applications. Today, you may use Heroku to run your web services, or you may manage a Hadoop cluster to execute MapReduce jobs. In these examples, Heroku and the Hadoop cluster are the platforms for web services and MapReduce jobs. A Mesos cluster can also be a platform for higher-level applications. But if your system already works, why add Mesos to the mix? Mesos offers flexibility and mitigates the risk of being outpaced by technology development; with Mesos, launching a Spark cluster or switching to a newer technology is as simple as launching the framework and watching it bootstrap itself.

Consider the Heroku/PaaS scenario: Marathon can reliably launch your application, automatically starting up new instances when machines crash or go down for maintenance. Mesos-DNS and HAProxy can manage your load balancing for you (see Chapter 3). But once you've got Mesos running, why bother continuing to maintain your Hadoop cluster? After all, you could launch Hadoop on Mesos via Myriad (*https://github.com/mesos/myriad*), and you could even stop dealing with HDFS administration, since there's a framework for that (Mesos HDFS (*https://github.com/mesosphere/hdfs*)).

Thus, you can think of Mesos as an execution platform: rather than paying for third-party PaaS solutions and creating bespoke clusters for each big data analysis technology, you can have a single Mesos cluster. With your Mesos cluster as the foundation, you can easily launch whatever frameworks you require to provide whatever functionality is needed, now or as new requirements and technologies arise.

How This Book Is Structured

At this point, let's take a look at how the rest of the book will be structured. First, we're going to learn about Mesos itself. We'll cover the architecture of Mesos and its frameworks, and we'll learn how resources are allocated across the cluster. We'll also dive into configuration settings you'll want to know, such as how to provide service-level agreements (SLAs) to certain frameworks, and useful command-line settings to tune the overall performance and workload of your cluster.

Then, we'll learn about two existing open source Mesos frameworks—Marathon and Chronos—that provide application hosting and job scheduling functionality. We'll explore how to configure them, how to interact with them, and how to build deeper integrations. After learning about these frameworks, you will be able to host several common application architectures, such as web services and data pipelines, on Mesos, with high reliability and scalability.

In the later parts of this book, we'll go into great detail about how to build a custom framework for Mesos. We'll learn about the APIs that it exposes through the process of implementing a sample job scheduling framework in Java. In developing this framework, we'll delve into how to build on the core Mesos APIs, what some common pitfalls are and how to avoid them, and how to decide whether to build a new framework or adapt an existing system.

At the end of the book, we'll do a deeper dive into some advanced features of Mesos, such as its integration with Docker, its internal architecture, and several cutting-edge APIs, including persistent disk management for databases and the framework reservation system.

Summary

In essence, Mesos is an operating system: it manages your computers and harnesses them together into a single, logical unit. Companies use Mesos because of the reliability, flexibility, and efficiency it brings. Mesos clusters require very few administrators to ensure that even massive fleets of machines remain operational.

Frameworks are distributed applications that run on Mesos; for them, Mesos provides infrastructure and execution services. Frameworks can act as applications, like Hadoop or Storm, or as deployment systems, like Ansible or Chef. Mesos coordinates and collaborates with frameworks to allocate slices of machines in the Mesos cluster to various roles. This capability—brokering the division of machines between many frameworks—is how Mesos enables greater operational efficiency.

With this high-level view of Mesos in mind, let's start diving into Mesos concepts and get started with Mesos in practice!

CHAPTER 2

Getting Started with Mesos

Now that you have a high-level understanding of the kinds of problems that Mesos can solve, let's dive in. What terminology is used by the project? How does Mesos manage resources? What structural constraints does Mesos impose on applications? By answering these questions and more, you'll develop the vocabulary and understanding to discuss Mesos. In subsequent chapters, we'll go into specifics about each technology, in order to develop applied skills in building applications with Mesos.

Frameworks

In the Mesos world, we assume that our distributed systems have a central controller and many workers. This is how most successful, scalable systems work: Google's BigTable, Apache Hadoop, and Twitter's Storm all have some sort of central controller that organizes their workers. Of course, the workers should be designed to work independently from the controller so that they're not bottlenecked by it and don't rely on it for their availability. Applications that run on Mesos are called *frameworks*. A framework has two parts: the controller portion, which is called the *scheduler*, and the worker portion, which are called the *executors*.

To run a framework on a Mesos cluster, we must run its scheduler. A scheduler is simply a process that can speak the Mesos protocol; frequently, our schedulers run on Marathon, but it's always necessary to consider how to ensure high availability for the scheduler. When a scheduler first starts up, it connects to the Mesos cluster so that it can use the cluster's resources. As the scheduler runs, it makes requests to Mesos to launch executors as it sees fit. This complete flexibility for the scheduler is what makes Mesos so powerful: schedulers can launch tasks based on resource availability, changing workloads, or external triggers. Today, there exist schedulers that can manage fleets of web services, schedulers that coordinate Storm topologies, and schedulers that optimize batch job placement.

When a scheduler wants to do some work, it launches an executor. The executor is simply the scheduler's worker: the scheduler then decides to send one or more *tasks* to the executor, which will work on those tasks independently, sending status updates to the scheduler until the tasks are complete. We'll learn more about the distinction between tasks and executors in "Tasks and Executors" on page 21.

Now that we've got an idea of what a framework is, let's take a step down the stack to learn about the Mesos cluster itself.

Masters and Slaves

A Mesos cluster is comprised of two components: the Mesos *masters* and the Mesos *slaves*. The masters are the software that coordinates the cluster; the slaves are what execute code in containers. You might be thinking, "That sounds awfully similar to how frameworks work."

In that case, you'd be 100% correct. The Mesos cluster mirrors the organization of the frameworks that run on top of it, because the master/slave pattern is simple, flexible, and effective. The cluster software needs to be separate, however, to ensure that frameworks remain isolated and secure from one another. First, we'll look at a few key ideas about the Mesos masters; then, we'll take a look at the slaves.

The Masters

The Mesos masters are the brain of the cluster. They have several responsibilities:

- They are the central source of truth for running tasks.
- They fairly share the cluster between all the connected frameworks.
- They host the primary UI for the cluster.
- They ensure high availability and efficient allocation of resources. Considered together, they are a single point of failure, but Mesos automatically handles and recovers from individual master failures.

Let's unpack these responsibilities, and see what they mean for the design of the masters and how they impact our clusters:

Masters are the central source of truth for all running tasks
    In order for masters to be able to serve the UI and data about tasks with minimal latency, all task metadata is kept in memory. This means that the nodes that run the masters should have plenty of memory—on a cluster with thousands of concurrent tasks, the masters could, for instance, consume 20 GB of RAM. Note that this excludes completed tasks, which relieves the memory pressure on the masters for some workloads. The masters make an effort to store the metadata related to recently completed tasks, but in the interest of saving memory, they

have a fixed-size buffer to store the last few hundred thousand tasks. On a very high throughput cluster, this could mean that completed task metadata is only available in the master for a few minutes. To retain task metadata for longer, you can use the Mesos monitoring system Satellite (*https://github.com/twosigma/satellite*) to automatically replicate the task metadata to a NoSQL database.

Masters fairly share the cluster between connected frameworks

The masters are responsible for offering resources to frameworks. Since the masters know exactly which frameworks are using which resources, they're able to determine which frameworks are using less than their share, and give those frameworks the first choice of free resources.[1] When configuring a Mesos cluster, you have many knobs for controlling the way resources are distributed amongst connected frameworks. Whenever a framework connects to Mesos, it connects with a role. Each role can have resources specifically set aside for it, and each role can be assigned a different weighted share of the remainder of the cluster. The administrators of the cluster can configure roles to ensure that each framework's SLA is met (see "Roles" on page 17).

Masters host the primary UI

When you want to use a browser to inspect and interact with the Mesos cluster, you'll typically first visit the master UI, which is on port 5050 by default. This UI allows you to see how many resources are available in total on your cluster, and how many are used. It allows you to see all of the connected frameworks, as well as information about them such as their framework ID and when they registered with Mesos. You can also see details about all of the current resource offers and tasks. The master UI automatically links each task with the UI of the slave that task is running on, so that you can even access files from the task's sandbox, such as its logs.

Masters ensure high availability

Mesos seeks to simplify building and running a highly available cluster. This is the reason that you should run three or five masters: as long as a majority of the masters are still running, the cluster can continue to operate as normal. The masters use the battle-tested Paxos (*http://bit.ly/paxoswiki*) algorithm to durably synchronize their beliefs about the status of the cluster. Since all masters have the same up-to-date view, any one of them can service and process requests. At the same time, Mesos seeks to enable building highly scalable clusters, which means being able to rapidly manage thousands of cluster allocations. To accomplish this, only one master is elected leader at a time. The leader is thus able to efficiently

---

1 Mesos uses a fair-sharing allocation algorithm called Dominant Resource Fairness (DRF). You can read about it in Ali Ghodsi et al.'s 2011 paper "Dominant Resource Fairness: Fair Allocation of Multiple Resource Types." (*https://www.cs.berkeley.edu/~alig/papers/drf.pdf*)

compute and make decisions about resource allocations, without being slowed down by waiting for the other masters on every decision. This design allows Mesos to achieve very high rates of scalable resource allocation, but still offer high availability in the face of partial failures. Of course, losing a majority of the masters does force the Mesos cluster to operate in a "safe mode"—when a majority of the masters are down, frameworks will not be able to allocate new resources or launch new tasks; however, running tasks will continue as normal. This means that even during a master outage, as long as the frameworks in use can continue to function without launching new tasks, the cluster as a whole can offer uninterrupted service even as individual components fail.

In this book, we won't cover how to install and run the Mesos masters and slaves: there are numerous tutorials on the Internet that cover exactly that, and they are customized for whatever operating system and deployment system you prefer.

The Slaves

Slave Will Be Renamed to Agent in Mesos 1.0

When Mesos reaches the 1.0 release, the nomenclature will change —the Mesos slave will be called the Mesos agent, and all occurences of "slave" will be changed to "agent."

The complement of the Mesos masters are the slaves. The slaves have a different set of responsibilities:

1. They launch and manage the containers that host the executors (both LXC containers and Docker images).

2. They provide a UI to access data from within the containers.

3. They communicate with their local executors in order to manage communications with the Mesos masters.

4. They advertise information about the hosts they're running on, including information about running tasks and executors, available resources, and other metadata.

5. They manage status updates from their tasks.

6. They checkpoint their state to enable rolling restarts of the cluster.

Let's break these down in turn:

Container management
    Mesos provides the best multitenancy isolation story for large clusters to date. It does so through the use of containerization technology. Containers are a light-

---

weight, extremely low-resource way to guarantee specific programs access to specific quantities of resources. For instance, a container could guarantee that a web server always can use 2 CPUs, 1 GB of RAM, and 500 MBps of network bandwidth, regardless of the demand of any other application on the machine. Mesos slaves have deep integration with LXC, the standard Linux Containers (*https://linuxcontainers.org/*) technology, as well as with Docker (*https://www.docker.com/*), the most popular packaging and containerization technology. Since the slaves need to be able to launch containers and ensure that the executors are run as specific users, the slave process typically runs as `root`,[2] so that it can create containers and run different executors as different users.

UI for slave-specific data

Just as the Mesos master UI exposes information about the state of the whole cluster, such as all the active tasks and frameworks, the slave UI exposes information about what's happening on a specific slave. Besides presenting a drilled-down version of the master UI (showing only frameworks, tasks, and executors that are related to that slave), the slave UI allows for interactive browsing of all the files within a container. This feature makes it easy to inspect the logs of any current or completed task, which is invaluable in debugging and monitoring the cluster. Frequently, Mesos framework UIs will link to the slaves' UIs, so that users can easily browse, view, and download the files produced by their tasks.

Communication with executors and masters

If you're reading this book, you've probably worked on distributed systems (or else you're about to). If that's the case, then you know (or will soon find out) that *distributed systems are hard*. In order to help us mere mortal programmers with these hard problems, the Mesos slave intermediates communications between executors and the masters. This means that every communication between executors and slaves is done locally, on a 100% reliable local loopback interface, which frees us from distributed systems reliability concerns.[3] Therefore, the Mesos slave can take responsibility for checkpointing and resynchronizing state during transient network problems or restarts, which helps to reduce the difficulty in building reliable worker applications.

Advertising information about their host

In Mesos, it is up to each slave to self-report the amount of resources it has available for running tasks. This design makes it trivial to add new capacity to a Mesos cluster: once a slave machine is started and the Mesos slave process connects to the masters, the slave chooses to communicate what resources it's mak-

---

2 It's possible to run a slave as a specific user, and then that Mesos slave can only run executors as that user. This can be useful in high-security environments or during development.

3 This isn't really true. Remember, distributed systems are hard!

ing available to the cluster. By default, the slave process will autodetect the CPUs, memory, and disks on the machine and expose them all to Mesos, available to any role. (The slave will reserve 1 GB or 50% of detected memory, whichever is smaller, in order to run itself and other operating system services. Likewise, it will reserve 5 GB or 50% of detected disk, whichever is smaller.) However, on the command line, you can specify exactly how many resources should be exposed, and whether any or all of those resources should be reserved for one or more roles. Besides the automatically detected resources, administrators can configure slaves to expose custom-defined resources, which we'll learn more about in "Configuring Custom Resources" on page 16. A slaves can also expose arbitrary key/value data about the machine (see "Configuring Slave Attributes" on page 17 for details). This is a great way to express information that might be useful to some schedulers, such as which rack the machine is on, what generation of processor features it supports, or what operating system it is running. By enhancing the advertised information that a slave shares with the cluster, you can add powerful features to your schedulers; for example, see "Using Placement Constraints" on page 38 to see how this data can enable rack-aware Marathon task placement.

Status updates

When a task sends a status update to its scheduler, it is guaranteed to be delivered at least once. It's the responsibility of the slave to store all status updates locally to disk, and periodically retransmit them if they aren't acknowledged by the task's scheduler. Without this, frameworks could fail to learn when their tasks complete during transient network or scheduler failures.

Rolling restarts

There's a tricky situation that arises when building an always-up distributed system: you need to be able to upgrade things without incurring any downtime. Typically, what you might try to do is restart a small fraction of your slaves at a time—that way, you never dip below 90% or 95% capacity. Unfortunately, there's a problem with this strategy. Consider the slaves on which you're running in-memory caches. Even if you restart them one at a time, it may take a long time to repopulate those caches, thus resulting in one of two choices: complete the slave upgrade faster, and suffer degraded application performance for far longer than the upgrade itself takes, or upgrade the slaves slowly and increase the time needed for the rolling upgrade by an order of magnitude or more. Mesos slaves have a feature called checkpointing, which gives us a third choice: the slave can periodically write snapshots of its own state plus the state of its tasks and executors, so that when you restart the slave process, rather than killing all of its tasks and executors, the new, upgraded version of the slave can simply read the checkpoint files and pick up where the previous version left off by reconnecting to the existing executors. This way, a rolling reboot of your slaves can be done quickly, and not a single task need die.

Using Cgroups on Mesos Slaves

Cgroups, a shortened name for *control groups*, are a way to group Linux processes together in order to do resource accounting and allocation. Every Mesos slave should have cgroups enabled, because they provide the CPU and memory isolation that ultimately makes Mesos so reliable. Processes on a Linux system belong to a node in the cgroup hierarchy; each node in the hierarchy has a certain share of the resources, and each child of a node has some subset of that node's resources. Through these resource hierarchies, anything from CPU shares and memory to network and disk I/O bandwidth can be accounted for and precisely shared. This sharing and accounting is what guarantees that one task can't starve another of resources. When the Mesos slave uses cgroups, it actually dynamically creates and destroys nodes in the hierarchy to match the allocations that the master calculates. This simplifies the administrators' jobs, since they need only ensure that cgroups have been enabled in the OS on the slave.

You can read about how to enable cgroups on the Debian wiki (*https:// wiki.debian.org/LXC*) and in the Red Hat Resource Management Guide (*http://red.ht/ 1T3Qu9k*). Mesos slaves will automatically work with Debian's and Red Hat 7's default cgroup instructions.

To enable cgroup isolation on the Mesos slaves, you must pass the command-line option `--isolation='cgroups/cpu,cgroups/mem'` to every slave. It is not recommended to use the default Posix isolator in production, as it doesn't provide the same robust isolation guarantees that the cgroups isolator does. Its primary purpose is to get process monitoring data when running Mesos for development purposes on a Mac.

Now we know the key responsibilities of the Mesos slave. The fundamental purpose of the slave is to expose the cluster's resources; in the next section, we'll learn what resources are and how to define custom resources.

Resources

The fundamental abstraction in Mesos is that of the resource—tasks and executors consume resources while performing their work. A common question is: "What is a resource?" The answer is broad: a resource is anything that a task or executor uses while doing its work. For example, the standard resources (and thus the resources that nearly every framework uses) are cpus, mem (memory), disk, and ports. The first three of those resources are scalar: they represent a total amount available, from which tasks deduct their usage. There are other resource types available in Mesos, as well. *Ranges* are lists of integers from which single elements or subranges can be allocated; for example, these are used to represent the ports available and in use. The last resource type, *sets*, are simply unordered collections of strings. We'll see an example of a set later on. First, let's learn about the standard resources:

cpus

This resource expresses how many CPU cores are available. Tasks may use fractional parts of a CPU—this is possible because Mesos slaves use CPU shares, rather than reserving specific CPUs. This means that, if you have 1.5 cpus reserved, your processes will be allowed to use a total of 1.5 seconds of CPU time each second. That could mean that, within a single executor, two processes each get 750 milliseconds of CPU time per second, or one process gets 1 second of CPU time and another gets 500 milliseconds of CPU time each in a given second. The benefit of using CPU shares is that if some task would be able to utilize more than its share, and no other task would use an otherwise idle CPU, the first task can potentially use more than its share. As a result, the cpus reserved provides a guaranteed minimum of CPU time available to the task—if additional capacity is available, it will be allowed to use more.

mem

mem is how many megabytes of memory are available. Unlike CPUs, which can burst to use more than their allocation if there's spare capacity, memory is a strictly preallocated resource. As a result, choosing the correct memory for tasks can be tricky: too little, and the tasks get killed when they try to allocate more than their allotment; too much, and memory sits idle that could otherwise be used for running more tasks.

disk

disk represents the amount of scratch space (in megabytes) that should be available in the container's sandbox. Since disk usage can be highly variable due to the unpredictability of errors filling up logs, many framework developers don't worry about reserving this resource in their tasks. Furthermore, by default, Mesos slaves don't even enforce when a task uses more disk than allocated. (To change that behavior, you can pass the option --enforce_container_disk_quota on your slaves' command lines. The other reason that this value is ignored is that the Mesos slaves automatically garbage collect the sandboxes of finished tasks when they need to reclaim disk space (see the following sidebar for details and advice on configuring garbage collection for slaves).

Configuring Slave Sandbox Garbage Collection

As tasks run on your Mesos cluster, they're sure to write data to disk. They can gener-ate logs, temporarily store output files, or cache their data or binaries. As mentioned, most Mesos users don't bother to enable the disk quota enforcement, since most disks are so big that it's unlikely a single job will fill them up. However, this logic works only in the short term. After days or weeks of running tasks, the sum of all the outputs of the tasks on a given machine will certainly exceed that slave's disk capacity. To solve this problem, Mesos slaves garbage collect old data from their disks. Let's look at the command-line options that configure the slave disk garbage collector (GC):

`--gc_delay`

> This option selects the maximum amount of time that an executor directory can exist before it is deleted. For example, it could be set to `--gc_delay=3days` or `--gc_delay=2weeks`; the default is `--gc_delay=1weeks`. Note that the system may shorten this delay, depending on the available disk usage.

`--disk_watch_interval`

> This option selects how often the disk usage is checked (and thus how often the GC will run). It uses the same time notation as the GC delay setting. For example, it could be set to `--disk_watch_interval=10secs`; the default value is `--disk_watch_interval=1mins`. If you set this to be too frequent, you could impact hard drive performance by enumerating directories too often.

`--gc_disk_headroom`

> This option selects what percentage of headroom, or free space, should be targe-ted by the GC. If you set the headroom too small, a task that writes to the disk too fast could consume all of the available space before the GC has time to run. On the flipside, if you set this too large, files will be garbage collected far earlier than necessary, which could make debugging annoying (e.g., if your data got deleted before you could look through it). The value of this option should be between 0.0 and 1.0; the default is `--gc_disk_headroom=0.1`, meaning that Mesos targets 10% of the disk as free space. The formula used to calculate the maximum age for an output directory is:
>
> `max_age = max (0.0, (1.0 – gc_disk_headroom – disk_usage))`

`ports`

> Ports are the first (and only default) nonscalar resource on Mesos slaves that we'll need to understand. Many tasks, such as HTTP servers, will want to open one or more ports, so that they can listen for incoming connections. Since each port can only be bound to one task, Mesos helps by allowing tasks to reserve specific

ports, so that each task uses a nonconflicting range. Furthermore, if a task *must* be bound to a particular port, then it can decline offers that don't include that port in the available range. By default, Mesos slaves expose ports 31000–32000; however, you can change this range by setting the `ports` resource to whatever you'd like on the command line.

Now that we've seen the basics of Mesos slave resources and learned about their default behaviors, let's learn how we can customize the resources offered.

Configuring Custom Resources

Perhaps you want to increase or decrease the resources set aside for operating system services. Maybe you need to expose additional ports, or ports within a particular range, in order to run a certain framework. Or possibly your slave machines have an exotic type of hardware, like a GPGPU, and you'd like to have Mesos manage the reservation and allocation of these devices. Finally, perhaps you'd like to reserve some of your resources to only be usable by a particular role. In any of these cases, you must provide a custom resource configuration to your Mesos slave.

Mesos resources are specified as key/value pairs. The *key* is the name of the resource: for example, `cpus`, `mem`, `disk`, or `ports`. The *value* is how many of those resources are available; the resource's type is determined by the value's syntax. Each resource is written as `key:value`; all the resources are concatenated together with semicolons and passed via the command line. Mesos supports scalar, set, and range resources. You can view the full grammar of resource attributes in the Mesos documentation (*http://mesos.apache.org/documentation/attributes-resources/*), but we'll go over a simple example.

Suppose that we'd like to have our slave advertise the following resources: 4.5 CPUs, 8 GB of RAM, the ports in the ranges of 1000–5000 and 31000–32000, and that it has 2 GPGPUs. Then, we'll have the following settings:

Resource	Value	Comments
cpus	4.5	Note that for scalar resources, you can provide a double.
mem	8192	Remember that memory is in MB.
ports	[1000-5000,31000-32000]	Ranges are written in square brackets; commas separate discontinuities.
gpgpus	{gpu1,gpu2}	Sets are written in curly braces; elements are separated by commas.

To pass this on the command line, we'd use the flag:

```
--resources='cpus:4;mem:8192;ports:[1000-5000;31000-32000];gpgpus:{gpu1,gpu2}'
```

All of the resources specified will belong to the default role.

Configuring Slave Attributes

Slaves can expose arbitrary key/value data about the machine as attributes. Unlike resources, attributes are not used by the Mesos allocator. They are merely passed along to framework schedulers to aid in their scheduling decisions. Suppose that you wanted to pass the following table of key/value pairs as attributes on the slave:

Key	Value
operating_system	ubuntu
cpu_class	haswell
zone	us_east
rack	22

To pass these attributes into the slave, we separate the keys and values with colons and separate the pairs with semicolons. This is the final command-line option pass:

```
--attributes='operating_system:ubuntu;cpu_class:haswell;zone:us_east;rack:22'
```

Roles

In order to decide which resources can be offered to which frameworks, Mesos includes the concept of "roles." A role is like a group: you can have the dgrnbrg role (for things you run), the qa role (for quality assurance-related tasks), the db role (for databases), and so on. Besides being used to exclusively reserve resources, roles also can be used to assign weights to Mesos's fair sharing algorithm. This allows you to specify that some roles should receive a greater ratio of resources on the cluster than others. When registering a framework, you may specify which role it belongs to by setting the role field in the FrameworkInfo message used to register. Frameworks will only receive offers that are for their role, or for the * role.

If you'd like to use roles, then you must include a comma-separated list of the valid roles on the master. For example, if you'd like to have dev, qa, and prod roles, then you'd need to pass --roles=dev,qa,prod to the master. To assign weights to those roles, so that dev gets twice as many offers as qa and prod gets three times as many offers as qa, you'd pass --weights='dev=2,qa=1,prod=3'.

Securing Roles

By default, any framework may claim to belong to any role. If necessary, roles can be secured through access control lists (ACLs), a security feature that is beyond the scope of this book. The `register_frameworks` ACL controls which roles each principal (aka user) can use when registering frameworks.

Static and Dynamic Slave Reservations

Slave reservations are the way to ensure that specific resources are always available for particular use cases. Until Mesos 0.25, only static reservations were available for operators. Now, there's also a dynamic API to reserve and unreserve resources without needing to change the command line.

Static reservations

Rather than only specifying which resources a slave exposes on its command line, we can also specify which roles can use those resources; this reserves those resources for a particular role. In the previous example, we didn't specify any roles for the resources; as a result, all the resources were assigned to the default role. The default role is set by the `--default_role` slave command-line option. If `--default_role` is unset, then the default role will be * (anyone).

To specify the role for a particular resource, we place the role name in parentheses after the resource. Let's suppose that we have a machine with 4 CPUs and 16 GB of RAM. We'd like to reserve 1 CPU and 4 GB of RAM for the role prod, and 2 CPUs and 1 GB of RAM for the role qa. The remainder of the resources should be able to be used by any user of the system. Then, we'll have the following settings:

Resource	Value	Role
cpus	1	prod
mem	4096	prod
cpus	2	qa
mem	1024	qa
cpus	13	*
mem	11264	*

To configure the slave, we can use the following command-line argument (note that this should all be typed on a single line, without the \ or any spaces; the command line has been wrapped here to fit in the page margins):

```
--resources='cpus(prod):1;mem(prod):4096; \
    cpus(qa):2;mem(qa):1024;cpus:13;mem:11264'
```

Note that we don't have to specify the role for the resources intended for *, since that's the default role. We could also change the default role to prod, and thus the command line would change:

```
--default_role=prod \
    --resources='cpus:1;mem:4096;cpus(qa):2;mem(qa):1024;cpus(*):13;mem(*):11264'
```

Note that changing the default role means that the autodetected disk and port ranges will also go to the prod role.

As you can see, slave reservations are a very powerful system that gives you control to ensure that production-critical workloads always receive a minimum allocation. At the same time, they're relatively tedious to configure and difficult to change, since they require changing the slave command line.

Dynamic reservations

As of Mesos 0.25, reservations can be created and destroyed via the /master/reserve and /master/unreserve HTTP endpoints. Let's look at how we'd reserve and unreserve the resources as shown in the previous section. For these examples, we'll assume that we've configured HTTP Basic authentication for a user principal admin, and that the appropriate ACLs have been configured. First we'll write some JSON, specifying the resources to reserve (see Example 2-1).

Example 2-1. resources.json

```
[
    {
        "name": "cpus",
        "type": "SCALAR", ❶
        "scalar": { "value": 1 },
        "role": "prod",
        "reservation": {
            "principal": "admin" ❷
        }
    },
    {
        "name": "mem",
        "type": "SCALAR",
        "scalar": { "value": 4096 },
        "role": "prod",
        "reservation": {
```

```
        "principal": "admin"
    }
},
{
    "name": "cpus",
    "type": "SCALAR",
    "scalar": { "value": 2 },
    "role": "qa",
    "reservation": {
        "principal": "admin"
    }
},
{
    "name": "mem",
    "type": "SCALAR",
    "scalar": { "value": 1024 },
    "role": "qa",
    "reservation": {
        "principal": "admin"
    }
}
}
```

❶ The HTTP API specifies resources the same way as the Mesos resource protobuf. See "Understanding mesos.proto" on page 23 to learn more about this structure.

❷ Dynamic reservations must be associated with a user, or *principal*. To make this reservation, we'll need to present the credentials of the admin user when we submit it.

To submit this reservation, we'll also need the slave ID of the slave on which we want to make this reservation (we'll use $SLAVEID in the example; a normal slave ID will look like 201509191529-2380865683-5050-11189-4621). Let's see how to combine our user credentials, *resources.json*, and slave ID into a curl command:

```
curl -u admin:password \ ❶
    -d slaveId=$SLAVEID\ ❷
    -d resources="$(cat resources.json)"\ ❸
    -X POST\ ❹
    http://<ip>:<port>/master/reserve ❺
```

❶ For this example, we assume that the admin user's password was set to password.

❷ We provide the slave ID and resources as key/value pairs to the endpoint.

❸ We will pass the resources in JSON format to curl. Note that the actual data that Mesos sees looks like slaveId=$SLAVEID&resources=$JSON.

❹ Both the /reserve and /unreserve endpoints require POSTing the data.

❺ We need to specify the URL of the Mesos master. This API makes reservations more convenient to configure, since you only need to interact with the master, rather than configuring each slave's reservation by interacting with that slave directly.

Destroying a reservation is almost identical to creating it:

```
curl -u admin:password \
    -d slaveId=$SLAVEID\
    -d resources="$(cat resources.json)"\
    -X POST\
    http://<ip>:<port>/master/unreserve ❶
```

❶ Note that the only thing we change is that we're now using the /unreserve endpoint. We still need to specify exactly which resources are being unreserved.

The new HTTP API for slave reservations promises to make ad hoc reservations much simpler to create, manage, and destroy. We should start to see tools to interact with this API at a higher level emerging as adoption increases (bear in mind that it was only released in October 2015).

Tasks and Executors

When a scheduler wants to do some work, it launches an *executor*. The executor is simply the scheduler's worker: the scheduler can decide to send one or more *tasks* to an executor, which will work on those tasks independently, sending status updates to the scheduler until the tasks are complete.

Up to this point, we haven't tried to distinguish the ideas of tasks and executors, because usually each executor has a single task, so there's not much point in differentiating between them. However, some frameworks leverage the full power of the task and executor abstraction, and to understand these frameworks we must understand the abstraction. For that we must first understand the problem: tasks are things that our scheduler wants to run in a container on a slave; however, we'd sometimes like to be able to run multiple tasks in the same container. For example, this pattern shows up with Storm workers and Hadoop TaskTrackers, each of which can contain many tasks.

So, what's an executor? An executor is a process container that runs tasks.

And what's a task? A task is the unit of work in Mesos.

Figure 2-1 illustrates the relationship between the elements of this abstraction.

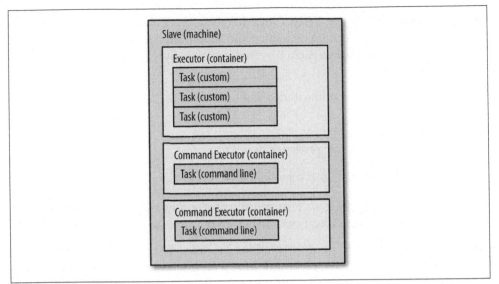

Figure 2-1. Relationship between slaves (machines), executors (containers), and tasks

There are also some caveats that you should be aware of:

Tasks can adjust the size of the executor's container
When you launch a task or executor in Mesos, both have resources attached to them. The reason for this is that an executor has a basic amount of resources that it requires for itself, and then each task can use additional resources. Mesos will automatically expand and contract the executor's container to have resources equal to the sum of those required by the executor plus all of its running tasks.

APIs can be task or executor oriented
When programming for the executor API (see Chapter 5 for details), some communication APIs between the executor and scheduler are are specified per task (such as `launchTask` and `statusUpdate`), whereas other APIs are per executor (such as `frameworkMessage`). It's up to the framework developers to make sure that they associate messages with tasks whenever necessary, regardless of whether the Mesos API does that automatically.

Most frameworks don't worry about distinguishing tasks and executors
Nearly every Mesos framework has one task for each executor. This means they don't need to worry about various idiosyncrasies in the executor APIs. Unfortunately, that in turn means that occasionally the executor APIs can be difficult to understand, since they see less use.

CommandExecutor

Most users and developers don't need to leverage the sophisticated features of the Mesos executor APIs. To assist rapid and reliable application development, Mesos comes with the CommandExecutor, which is a special, simplified executor. If your task simply launches a command-line application (and optionally downloads it from a location in storage) or a Docker image, you can specify a CommandInfo when launching a task, rather than an ExecutorInfo. If you do this, then Mesos will launch the specified command with the built-in CommandExecutor, which will handle the Mesos messaging protocol for you. Many frameworks, such as Chronos and Marathon, often use the CommandExecutor for its simplicity.

Understanding mesos.proto

Throughout this book and your own development efforts, you'll often wonder how you configure some API or what the configuration options are for some feature. All communication with Mesos is encoded in Google Protocol Buffers (*https://develop ers.google.com/protocol-buffers/*) (commonly known as *protobufs*). Lucky for us, all of the data schemas are stored in a central location: the file *include/mesos/mesos.proto* in the Mesos codebase (*https://github.com/apache/mesos*). Let's take a tour of Google protobufs, and learn some idioms that frequently show up in the Mesos codebase.

Protobufs is an interface description language that allows an application's developers to specify strongly typed messages that exist in their system. Many languages have protobuf compilers, which convert *.proto* files into efficient serializers and deserializers so that all of the languages can communicate with an efficient binary encoding.

First, let's learn the basics of protobufs:

```
/** ❶
 *  This represents information about a user.
 *  We'll respect their privacy as much as possible.
 */
message UserInfo { ❷
  // The name of the user ❸
  required string username = 1; ❹
  required Name name = 2; ❺
  optional uint32 age = 4; ❻
  // Auxiliary info
  optional bytes aux_info = 3; ❼
}

message Name { ❽
  optional string first = 1; ❾
  optional string last = 2;

  message MiddleName { ❿
```

```
    optional string regular = 1;  ⑪
    optional string patronymic = 2;
  }

  repeated MiddleName middle = 3;  ⑫

  optional uint32 total_parts = 4 [default = 2];  ⑬
}
```

❶ Protobufs supports block comments in the style of JavaDocs.

❷ The main syntactic form in a *.proto* file is the `message`, which has a name (`UserInfo`) and a set of typed, named fields.

❸ Protobufs also supports comments that span to the end of the line, like C and Java.

❹ A field has four parts: whether is it `required`, `optional`, or `repeated`; the type (`string`, in this case); the name of the field; and the field index. Each field index must be unique to the message; it is the developer's responsibility to never reuse the indices, because they are the foundation on which backward compatibility in the binary format is built.

❺ A field's type can itself be another `message`.

❻ Protobufs has many built-in numeric types; Mesos primarily uses `int32`, `uint32`, and `double`. Also, notice that the field indices don't have to be in numeric order—they're usually grouped to reflect the structure of the message.

❼ `bytes` allows you to store arbitrary binary data in a protobuf. In Mesos's protobuf messages, this is used to enable developers to define custom additional payloads.

❽ Generally, most or all of a project's messages are defined in a single file.

❾ You don't *need* to make any fields `required`.

❿ Messages can be nested into other messages.

⑪ Note that the field numbering restarts within every message, even nested messages.

⑫ Fields can also be repeated, in which case they're a list of zero or more entries of the specified type (in this case, `MiddleName`).

⑬ Protobufs allows default values to be specified.

Besides the basics, there are a few patterns that frequently show up in *mesos.proto*. Firstly, any ID in the system typically has a message defined for it, with only a single required string value (c.f. `FrameworkID`, `TaskID`). This is beneficial for typed languages like C++, Scala, and Java, because it ensures that different types of IDs can't get mixed up. Secondly, when there is a choice for what to specify (for instance, a custom executor vs. a command executor), both choices are made `optional`, and there should be a comment in *mesos.proto* that explains the choice. Most messages that can be generated by framework code have a `data` field of type `bytes`: this is the place to put any serialized messages or data you may want to transmit.

The Browser Tab I Never Close

Given the reliance on comments for this pattern, I always have *mesos.proto* open when I'm developing framework code.

Another common pattern in *mesos.proto* is *tagged unions*. A tagged union is also known as a *discriminated union*; it is used when there are multiple mutually exclusive choices for how to configure something. Unions of this type, such as the `Resource` message, have every choice `optional`, so that you can fill in just one per message. There is also a required `Type` field, which indicates to the code which field you intended to specify. For example, to specify a scalar resource, the `Type` of the resource should be `SCALAR` and the `scalar` field should contain the value.

Finally, *mesos.proto* is usually where new features of Mesos are specified and incubated. As a result, you'll often see upcoming features described in *mesos.proto* without other official documentation. For example, the service discovery system and the persistent volumes features were in *mesos.proto* for several releases prior to becoming stable, supported features in Mesos. *mesos.proto* can give you a lot of insight into what's coming up for Mesos; however, it can be confusing and overwhelming if you don't ignore messages and fields unrelated to your task at hand.

Not Managed by Mesos

To have a functional Mesos cluster, you'll need a few other applications that are difficult or impossible to run as frameworks:

ZooKeeper

Mesos uses ZooKeeper (*https://zookeeper.apache.org/*) to provide discovery services across your cluster. ZooKeeper quorums are named by the DNS names of the machines that they run on; as a result, the Mesos cluster's ZooKeeper quorum usually runs on three or five specific machines, so that it can have a stable name.

Databases

Initial support for persistent volumes was only recently added, in Mesos version 0.23. As a result, most databases don't yet have mature Mesos frameworks. Nevertheless, work is rapidly progressing on hosting databases on Mesos. Twitter has been developing Apache Cotton (previously called Mysos), which runs and manages MySQL on Mesos, since 2014. Mesosphere has also been working with its partners to productionalize Cassandra and Kafka on Mesos, and Basho has released a beta version of a Riak framework for Mesos, which includes a high-performance proxy layer that was enabled by Mesos.

Monitoring

Mesos watches and monitors its frameworks, which helps developers build highly available and reliable systems. But, in the loosely translated words of the Roman poet Juvenal, "Who watches the watchers?" Mesos itself needs to be monitored; it collects instantaneous usage and utilization data, but that data should be archived and graphed to understand the cluster's behavior over time. In addition, Mesos isn't built to identify issues with the machines that it's running on. Thus, a robust, productionalized Mesos cluster should have host-level monitoring, and it should archive and alert on data collected by Mesos itself. One integrated solution to this is Satellite (*https://github.com/twosigma/satellite*), which can automatically disable flaky slaves, generate alerts on custom conditions, and store historical data to InfluxDB, ElasticSearch, and many other databases.

Luckily, setting up a monitoring system and one ZooKeeper cluster involves a lot less work than setting up standalone versions of all the frameworks that we're going to run on Mesos!

Summary

A Mesos cluster is comprised of the masters, which coordinate the cluster, and the slaves, which execute tasks on behalf of frameworks. The master/slave structure of the Mesos cluster is mirrored by the frameworks, which are each composed of a scheduler that controls executors, which run on the slaves.

Mesos slaves can be customized with additional key/value metadata, custom resource types, and roles, which are all ways to ensure that framework schedulers can choose the best slaves on which to run their executors, and to help the administrators to guarantee the allocation behaviors of the Mesos masters. The master and slave states can be browsed through web UIs that cross-reference data across the cluster.

Executors are the processes that actually run inside of containers on the slaves. In Mesos, executors can host one or more tasks, which provides flexibility for framework authors to structure their applications however they'd like; however, most frameworks use the `CommandExecutor` to run one task per executor (i.e., one task per container).

Finally, although Mesos provides a lot of functionality, one still must deploy certain tools outside of Mesos: specifically, a ZooKeeper quorum to bootstrap the cluster, a monitoring system, and possibly some databases.

Now that we've had a tour of Mesos, let's learn how to port an existing web application onto Mesos!

CHAPTER 3

Porting an Existing Application to Mesos

It's time to learn how to build an application on top of Mesos. Rather than building everything from first principles, however, let's take a look how to utilize existing frameworks to port our legacy applications. When we think about most applications, they typically fall into two categories: applications that respond to requests and applications that do actions at a particular time. In the LAMP stack (*http://bit.ly/LAMP wiki*), these two components are PHP and cron jobs.

First, we're going to look at how to move an existing HTTP-based application from your current infrastructure onto Mesos. In doing so, we're going to begin to be able to take advantage of Mesos's scalability and resiliency, ending up with a system that can automatically heal and recover from common failure classes. Besides improving the resiliency of the application, we're also going to improve the isolation of the application's components. This will help us to achieve a better quality of service without struggling and suffering to build this directly on virtual machines. We'll use Marathon, a popular Mesos framework, to host our HTTP-based application.

Then, we'll look at Chronos as a case study in using Marathon to add high availability and reliability to other frameworks. Chronos will enable us to run programs at a specified interval—it can be used to schedule nightly data generation jobs or reports every 15 minutes. We'll also go over some recommendations for utilizing Chronos effectively and maintainably.

Finally, we'll briefly touch on some alternatives to Marathon, Singularity and Aurora, which were developed by HubSpot and Twitter, respectively.

Moving a Web Application to Mesos

Nearly every company has a web application. However, no matter whether it's written in Ruby on Rails, Scala Play!, or Python's Flask, deploying it in a reliable, scalable, highly available manner is always a challenge. In this section, we're going to learn about using Marathon—an easy-to-use Platform as a Service (PaaS) developed by Mesosphere—and how to integrate with other tools, such as HAProxy. Through this process, it is our goal to realize a few benefits over previous architectures:

1. All of our backend processes will be able to run on any machine, and our Mesos framework will handle automatically spinning up new instances of the backend when existing instances fail.

2. We will host our static assets, fast-responding endpoints, dangerous endpoints,[1] and API in entirely different containers to improve our isolation.

3. We will make it easy to deploy a new version or to roll back, and to do so in a matter of seconds.

4. We will put the pieces in place to allow our applications to autoscale based on demand.

At its core, Marathon allows you to specify a command line or Docker image, number of CPUs, amount of memory, and number of instances, and it will start that many instances of that command line or image in containers with the requested amount of CPU and memory. We will explore this basic configuration as well as a few ways to integrate Marathon with load balancers, in order to expose our services internally and to the outside world.

Setting Up Marathon

Obviously, in order to use Marathon, you'll need to download it. Marathon comes prepackaged for Ubuntu, Debian, Red Hat, and CentOS on the Mesosphere website (*https://mesosphere.com/downloads/*). Of course, you can also build it yourself, by downloading the latest tarball from Mesosphere's website, or by cloning it from Git-Hub (*https://github.com/mesosphere/marathon*). Marathon is written in Scala, so you simply need to run `sbt assembly` to build it. From here on out, we'll assume that you've got a copy of Marathon installed.

Marathon is trivial to run as a highly available application. In fact, all you need to do to run Marathon in a highly available configuration is to ensure that you start two or three instances of Marathon, and that they all share the same `--zk` command-line argument. You should also make other options the same, such as the `--master`, `--framework-name`, and the ports that it listens for HTTP requests on, or you could see confusing behavior. When running Marathon in this mode, all the instances of

---

1 By this, I mean endpoints that may result in running a query on the database or making an external service call that you can't predict how long it will take, or whether we'll consume resources indefinitely.

Marathon will correctly respond to requests, and they'll magically synchronize their state so that you don't need to worry about this. Typically, you'll finish the setup by assigning the instances of Marathon to a round-robin DNS name, or putting it behind a load balancer. Please see Table 3-1 for further information on selected command-line options.

Table 3-1. Selected Marathon command-line options

Flag	Functionality
`--master <instance>`	The URL of the Mesos master. Usually of the form `zk://host1:port,host2:port,host3:port/mesos`.
`--framework-name <name>`	Allows you to customize the name of this instance of Marathon in Mesos; useful if you have multiple instances of Marathon running to stay organized.
`--zk <instance>`	Sets the instance of ZooKeeper in which Marathon's state is stored. Usually of the form `zk://host1:port,host2:port,host3:port/marathon`.
`--https-port <port>`	Enables HTTPS access to Marathon. See "Securing Marathon and Chronos" on page 31 for details.

Securing Marathon and Chronos

In this sidebar, we'll go over how to secure Marathon and Chronos by requiring authentication before making any changes to them, and ensuring all API communications are protected with SSL. Although many organizations run Marathon and Chronos within their trusted networks, others will need to apply access restrictions to ensure that only authorized users can view or make changes to the running jobs. Note that this will not secure the connection between Marathon or Chronos and Mesos; to do that, you'll need to configure `--mesos_authentication_principal` and `--mesos_authentication_secret_file` for the Mesos authentication scheme you've chosen. This is useful to guard against someone accidentally deleting or changing a production-critical service, or a rogue employee acting maliciously.

All of these security settings can be configured either with environment variables or with command-line options. You should use the environment variables, because the command-line options will enable anyone logged into the machine running Marathon or Chronos to see the passwords by running `ps -f`. The environment variables can be protected by having the script that starts the application `export` all the sensitive environment variables before launching. The launcher script can have the permissions set to be unreadable to most users on the machine, which is how you'll secure those passwords.

Chronos and Marathon are built on top of the same HTTP/REST services library, which is named Chaos. Chaos currently only supports HTTP Basic authentication, also known as username/password authentication. To set the `username:password` pair, you should format them as such (separated by a colon). You can pass them as a command-line argument via:

```
--http_credentials username:password
```

or as an environment variable via:

```
MESOSPHERE_HTTP_CREDENTIALS=username:password
```

HTTP authentication is not terribly useful on its own, however, because anyone could listen to the connection between the client and server to recover the password. To prevent this, you can enable SSL as well. Because Chaos is a Java application, it needs to use the Java certificate file format, known as a keystore (*http://en.wikipedia.org/wiki/Keystore*). The keystore is a password-protected container for the SSL certificate. To configure this, you specify the path to the keystore on the command line via:

```
--ssl_keystore_path /path/to/keystore
```

or as an environment variable via:

```
MESOSPHERE_KEYSTORE_PATH=/path/to/keystore
```

You'll also need to provide the password. You can do this on the command line via:

```
--ssl_keystore_password password
```

or as an environment variable via:

```
MESOSPHERE_KEYSTORE_PASS=password
```

At this point, you are probably thinking, "Why does Java have to do everything differently? Why can't it just be compatible with normal certificates?" Luckily, it's easy to convert a standard PEM-format PKCS12 certificate (such as the type most Certificate Authorities issue) into a keystore. To do this, you'll need your key (*mykey.pem*) and certificate (*mycert.pem*). First, you'll make a combined file (*mykeycert.pem*) by running:

```
cat mykey.pem mycert.pem > mykeycert.pem
```

Then, you'll use `openssl` to create the keystore (*mykeystore.pkcs12*) containing this certificate. Strangely, keystores require all certificates that they store to have "aliases." Our certificate will be called `myalias`. Without further ado, here's the command:

```
openssl pkcs12 -export -in mykeycert.pem -out mykeystore.pkcs12 \
    -name myalias -noiter -nomaciter
```

And voilà! You can now use any standard issue certificate to secure Marathon and Chronos.

Make sure to disable the HTTP access once you've done this though, or you'll have put a lock on the front door but left the back door wide open! This can be done with the command-line argument `--disable_http` to Marathon and Chronos.

Using Marathon

Marathon is controlled entirely through its HTTP API. With a working instance of Marathon, let's try launching an application.

We'll run a simple application: the famous Python `SimpleHTTPServer`. This application simply serves the files in the directory in which it was started. We're going to base our example on it because nearly everyone's got Python installed, and it's available by default.

If you run this command:

```
python -m SimpleHTTPServer 8000
```

on your computer, then you should be able to navigate to `localhost:8000` in your browser and see a directory listing of the folder in which you started the server.

Let's see how we can run that on a Marathon server running on `marathon.example.com:8080`. We'll first make a file containing the JSON descriptor of the Marathon application shown in Example 3-1.

Example 3-1. SimpleHTTPServer JSON descriptor

```
{
    "cmd": "python -m SimpleHTTPServer 31500", ❶
    "cpus": 0.5, ❷
    "mem": 50, ❸
    "instances": 1, ❹
    "id": "my-first-app", ❺
    "ports": [31500], ❻
    "requirePorts": true ❼
}
```

❶ The `"cmd"` specifies the command line that will launch your application.

❷ `"cpus"` specifies the number of CPUs that your application's container should have. This number can be fractional.

❸ `"mem"` specifies the number of MB of memory that your application's container should have.

❹ `"instances"` specifies how many copies of this application should be started on the cluster. For this demo, we'll only make one instance, but typical applications will have anywhere from 2 to 2,000 instances.

❺ `"id"` is how we'll refer to this application in the future via the APIs. This should be unique for each application.

⑥ `"ports"` is an array of the ports that the application requires. In this case, we only need a single port. Later, we'll see how to dynamically allocate and bind to ports.

⑦ Since we're explicitly specifying which ports we want to allocate, we must tell Marathon, or else it will default to automatic port assignment.

Now let's suppose that data has been stored in a file called *my-first-app.json*. In order to start this application, we'll use an HTTP POST to send the data to a Marathon server running at `marathon.example.com:8080`:

```
curl -X POST -H 'Content-Type: application/json' \
    marathon.example.com:8080/v2/apps --data @my-first-app.json
```

This should give us a response that looks something like:

```
{
    // This section contains parameters we specified
    "id" : "/my-first-app",
    "instances" : 1,
    "cmd" : "python -m SimpleHTTPServer 31500",
    "ports" : [ 31500 ],
    "requirePorts": true,
    "mem" : 50,
    "cpus" : 0.5,

    // This section contains parameters with their automatically assigned values
    "backoffFactor" : 1.15,
    "maxLaunchDelaySeconds" : 3600,
    "upgradeStrategy" : {
        "minimumHealthCapacity" : 1,
        "maximumOverCapacity" : 1
    },
    "version" : "2015-06-04T18:26:18.834Z",
    "deployments" : [
        {
            "id" : "54e5fdf8-8a81-4f95-805f-b9ecc9293095"
        }
    ],
    "backoffSeconds" : 1,
    "disk" : 0,
    "tasksRunning" : 0,
    "tasksHealthy" : 0,
    "tasks" : [],
    "tasksStaged" : 0,

    // This section contains unspecified parameters
    "executor" : "",
    "storeUrls" : [],
    "dependencies" : [],
    "args" : null,
    "healthChecks" : [],
```

```
        "uris" : [],
        "env" : {},
        "tasksUnhealthy" : 0,
        "user" : null,
        "requirePorts" : true,
        "container" : null,
        "constraints" : [],
        "labels" : {},
    }
```

which indicates that the application was started correctly.

We can find all the information about the running application by querying for information about my-first-app (what we decided to name this application):

```
curl marathon.example.com:8080/v2/apps/my-first-app | python -m json.tool
```

This query returns almost the exact same data as we got when we created the application. The difference is that by now our application has had time to start running, so we can see information about the running tasks:

```
// ... snip (same as before) ...
    "tasks": [
        {
            "appId": "/my-first-app",
            "host": "10.141.141.10", ❶
            "id": "my-first-app.7345b7b5-0ae7-11e5-b3a7-56847afe9799", ❷
            "ports": [ 31500 ], ❸
            "stagedAt": "2015-06-04T18:28:09.235Z", ❹
            "startedAt": "2015-06-04T18:28:09.404Z", ❺
            "version": "2015-06-04T18:28:05.214Z" ❻
        }
    ],
    "tasksHealthy" : 1, ❼
// ... snip (same as before) ...
```

❶ This tells us the DNS name or IP address of the host that is running the task.

❷ The id of the task is a Mesos construct. We can use the Mesos master's UI to inspect this task; for instance, we can examine its stdout and stderr.

❸ Whether we chose the port that the application is running on or allowed Marathon to choose for us (see Example 3-2 for details), we can find the actually reserved ports for the task.

❹ The staging time of the task is when we submitted the task to a Mesos offer.

❺ The start time of the task is when Mesos actually got around to launching the task.

❻ Every time we update the Marathon descriptor, it gets stamped with a new version (see the response to the initial `POST` given earlier). Every task is annotated with the version from which it was launched.

❼ This gives a summary of the number of currently healthy tasks in the application.

Let's look at some of the rich information available about the application. First, we can see all of the configuration parameters that we specified when we created the application. We also see tons and tons of other settings, many of which we'll go over soon. The next very interesting field is `"tasks"`, which is an array of all of the actual running instances of the application. Each task is represented as a JSON object, which has several useful fields:

- `"host"` and `"ports"` tell us what the actual host and ports that were assigned to this task are. These fields are the key to discovering where an application is actually running so that we can connect to it.

- `"id"` is the mesos `TaskID`. This is constructed by adding a unique per-task UUID to the application's ID, which allows for convenient discovery with the Mesos CLI tools or in the Mesos UI.

- `"stagedAt"` and `"startedAt"` give us information about when lifecycle events happened to this task. A task is *staged* once Marathon actually requests Mesos to start the task on a particular offer; a task is *started* once it begins running.

Upcoming Change in Marathon REST API

The REST API examples in this book are valid as of Marathon 0.9. In the future, Marathon will filter the results so requests don't need to return megabytes of JSON data. When this happens, you'll need to specify an additional, repeatable URL parameter: `embed`. That is, instead of `/v2/apps/my-first-app`, you need to request `/v2/apps/my-first-app?embed=app.counts&embed=app.tasks` to retrieve the data for the preceding examples. You can read about all of the options for `embed` in the Marathon REST API documentation (*https://mesosphere.github.io/marathon/docs/rest-api.html*).

Usually, you won't want to hardcode the port for your application: after all, if you did this, then you'd only ever be able to run one instance of the application per slave. Marathon can specify the port for you, instead: simply choose each port your application requires as `0`, and the assigned ports will be available in the environment variables `$PORT0`, `$PORT1`, etc. If we changed our earlier configuration to take advantage of this, we'd end up with Example 3-2.

Example 3-2. SimpleHTTPServer JSON descriptor with dynamically chosen port

```
{
    "cmd": "./python -m SimpleHTTPServer $PORT0", ❶
    "cpus": 0.5,
    "mem": 50,
    "instances": 1,
    "id": "my-first-app",
    "ports": [0], ❷
    "uris": [
        "http://fetchable/uri/with/python.tar.gz" ❸
    ]
}
```

❶ Note that we use $PORT0 to access the environment variable that contains the port assigned to the first index of the "ports" array.

❷ We provided 0 as the desired port, meaning that we're allowing Marathon to choose for us.

❸ We can also provide a list of URIs to be fetched and unzipped into the container before running the command. See "Configuring the process's environment" on page 94 for details on the URI schemes supported.

Some applications you'd like to run on Marathon don't accept their ports via the command line. Don't worry! There's an easy way for us to propagate our $PORT0 environment variables into configuration files. I'll assume that the application's configuration file is set as a URL to be downloaded with the application. Now, we're going to use sed to replace a special string in the configuration file with the desired environment variable, be it a $PORT0 or the $MESOS_DIRECTORY:

```
sed -e 's#@MESOSDIR@#'"$MESOS_DIRECTORY"'#' config.templ > config ❶
sed -e 's#@PORT@#'"$PORT0"'#' config2.templ > config2 ❷
```

❶ In our first example, we are replacing the string @MESOSDIR@ with the task's sandbox directory. We surround the string in the configuration file with @ symbols, because they so rarely show up in configuration languages (of course, you could use any unique string). Also, we use single quotes around the "constants" in our sed command and double quotes around the environment variable to ensure that our shell doesn't corrupt our command. Finally, we use # instead of / for the sed command so that we can successfully template an environment variable that itself contains forward slashes.

❷ Here, we template the port at index 0 into the configuration file. In fact, we could pass multiple -e arguments to a single invocation of sed if we wanted to template several variables in one configuration file.

We'll look at other fields as we cover the features that utilize them.

Scaling Your Application

Let's see what it would take to scale our HTTP server to have five instances. Ready?

```
curl -X PUT -H 'Content-Type: application/json' \
    marathon.example.com:8080/v2/apps --data '{"instances": 5}'
```

Of course, no one would ever actually want to have five instances of such a useless application, so why don't we scale it down?

```
curl -X PUT -H 'Content-Type: application/json' \
    marathon.example.com:8080/v2/apps --data '{"instances": 1}'
```

Luckily, scaling is extremely easy!

Using Placement Constraints

Marathon supports constraints on where the application is launched. These constraints can be driven either by the hostname of the slave or any slave attribute. Constraints are provided in an array to the application; each constraint is itself an array of two or three elements, depending on whether there's an argument. Let's take a look at what constraints are available and how to use them:

GROUP_BY
> This operator ensures that instances of the application are evenly spread across nodes with a particular attribute. You can use this to spread the application equitably across hosts (Example 3-3) or racks (assuming that the rack is encoded by the rack attribute on the slave; see Example 3-4).
>
> *Example 3-3. Spread evenly by host*
>
> ```
> {
>     // ... snip ...
>     "constraints": [["hostname", "GROUP_BY"]]
> }
> ```
>
> *Example 3-4. Spread evenly by rack*
>
> ```
> {
>     // ... snip ...
>     "constraints": [["rack", "GROUP_BY"]]
> }
> ```

UNIQUE
> This operator ensures that every instance of the application has a different value for the UNIQUE constraint. It's similar to GROUP_BY, except if there are not enough

---

different values for the attribute, the application will fail to fully deploy, rather than running multiple instances on some slaves. Usually, GROUP_BY is the best choice for availability, since it's generally preferable to have multiple tasks running on a single slave rather than fewer than the desired number. Example 3-5 shows how you could use UNIQUE to ensure that there's no more than one instance of some application per slave in the cluster.

Example 3-5. Run at most one instance per host

```
{
    // ... snip ...
    "constraints": [["hostname", "UNIQUE"]]
}
```

CLUSTER

This operator allows you to run an application only on slaves with a specific value for an attribute. If certain slaves have special hardware configurations, or if you want to restrict placement to a specific rack, this operator can be useful; however, LIKE is more powerful and often a better fit. For example, suppose that we've got a mixture of ARM and x86 processors in our data center, and we've made a cpu_arch attribute for our slaves to help us distinguish their architectures. Example 3-6 shows how to ensure that our application only runs on x86 processors.

Example 3-6. Only run on x86

```
{
    // ... snip ...
    "constraints": [["cpu_arch", "CLUSTER", "x86"]] ❶
}
```

❶   Note that the CLUSTER operator takes an argument.

LIKE

This operator ensures that the application runs only on slaves that have a certain attribute, and where the value of that attribute matches the provided regular expression. This can be used like CLUSTER, but it has more flexibility, since many values can be matched. For example, suppose that we're running on Amazon, and we set the instance_type attribute on all of our slaves. Example 3-7 shows how we could restrict our application to run only on the biggest C4 compute-optimized machines.

Example 3-7. Only run on c4.4xlarge and c4.8xlarge machines

```
{
    // ... snip ...
    "constraints": [["cpu_arch", "LIKE", "c4.[48]xlarge"]] ❶
}
```

❶ LIKE's argument is a regular expression.

UNLIKE

UNLIKE is the complement of LIKE: it allows us to avoid running on certain slaves. Maybe you don't want some daemons (such as ones processing user billing information) to run on machines that are in the DMZ, which is an unsecured network area. By setting the attribute dmz to true on machines in the DMZ, we can have our application avoid those machines, as in Example 3-8.

Example 3-8. Don't run in the DMZ

```
{
    // ... snip ...
    "constraints": [["dmz", "UNLIKE", "true"]] ❶
}
```

❶ UNLIKE's argument can be a regular expression.

Placement constraints can also be combined. For example, we could ensure that our application isn't running in the DMZ and is evenly distributed amongst the remaining machines as shown in Example 3-9.

Example 3-9. Combining constraints

```
{
    // ... snip ...
    "constraints": [["dmz", "UNLIKE", "true"],
                    ["hostname", "GROUP_BY"]]
}
```

Combining constraints will allow you to precisely control how your applications are placed across the cluster.

Running Dockerized Applications

Marathon has first-class support for Docker containers. If your app is already Dockerized, then it's very easy to run it on Marathon.

In order to get started, you'll first need to make sure that your Mesos cluster has Docker support enabled. To do this, make sure that you've enabled the Docker containerizer and increased the executor timeout (see "Using Docker" on page 129 for details).

At this point, we can simply add the Docker configuration to the JSON that we use to configure our application. Let's take a look at the options we have when using Docker, as illustrated in Example 3-10. Note that this JSON configuration is partial; it must also include additional options such as those in Example 3-1.

Example 3-10. Marathon Docker JSON configuration

```
{
    // ... snip ...
    "container": {
        "type": "DOCKER", ❶
        "docker": {
            "image": "group/image", ❷
            "network": "HOST" ❸
        }
    }
}
```

❶ Since Mesos will continue to add new container types, such as Rocket or KVM containers, much of the container configuration isn't Docker-specific. Here, we must specify that we'll provide Docker-specific configuration, because this is a DOCKER container.

❷ This is the most important part: where you specify your container image.[2]

❸ We're going to run Docker in host networking mode; this means that Docker is using the slave's networking resources directly.

Once the Docker container launches, it'll also have access to the Mesos sandbox directory, which will be available in the environment variable $MESOS_SANDBOX.

Mounting host volumes

Often, when using Docker, you may want to mount some volume available on the host. This may be some globally distributed configuration files, data files, or maybe you'd just like a data directory that won't be automatically garbage collected. Example 3-11 shows how to add this to the JSON configuration.

---

2 If you'd like to use a private Docker repository, you can add the *.dockercfg* to the "uris" field of the application descriptor, as described in the Advanced Docker Configuration note in the section "Using Docker" on page 129.

Example 3-11. Mounting host volumes

```
{
    "container": {
        "type": "DOCKER",
        "docker": {
            "image": "group/image",
            "network": "HOST"
        },
        "volumes": [ ❶
            { ❷
                "containerPath": "/var/hostlib",
                "hostPath": "/usr/lib",
                "mode": "RO" ❸
            },
            { ❹
                "containerPath": "/var/scratch",
                "hostPath": "/mount/ssd",
                "mode": "RW"
            }
        ]
    }
}
```

❶ Note that the "volumes" aren't considered Docker-specific, and you can specify an array of them.

❷ This volume allows us to access the */usr/lib* directory of the host machine from within our Docker container. This could be useful if we'd like to access *libmesos.so* from the host, rather than needing to keep updating our Docker image.

❸ We can mount the volume in read-only (RO) or read-write (RW) mode.

❹ This volume gives us some SSD-mounted scratch space, assuming that an SSD is mounted at */mount/ssd* on the host.

Mounting host volumes into the Docker container might seem like a great way to host databases on Marathon; after all, you can provide persistent host storage to containers. Unfortunately, even though you can mount volumes with Docker, there are a few reasons why this is very hard (at least, until Mesos natively supports volumes). First of all, it's tedious to communicate which machines have disks available. In order to accomplish this, you'll need to use placement constraints to ensure all of the following:

1. Each slave with a spare volume has a special attribute identifying it as having that volume, so that you can use the CLUSTER operator to ensure placement on those slaves.

2. The application has the UNIQUE operator set on the hostname, so that only one instance of the application launches on each slave (since there's only one special mount point per machine).

3. Every one of the slaves has its host volume mounted on the same path (luckily, this is the easiest part).

If you feel up to the task, this can help you to get certain types of databases running on Marathon. Sadly, you won't have scaling or automatic recovery handled for you, since there's so much special configuration necessary on each slave. Happily, as Mesos adds support for persistent disks, more and more specialized frameworks that handle launching and configuring databases will pop up, and this mess will no longer be needed.

Health Checks

Marathon keeps track of whether it believes an application is healthy or not. This information is exported via the REST API, making it easy to use Marathon to centralize management of its application health checks. When you query the REST API for information about a particular application, all of its tasks will include their latest health check results. By default, Marathon assumes that a task is healthy if it is in the RUNNING state. Of course, just because an application has started executing doesn't mean that it's actually healthy. To improve the usefulness of the application's health data, you can specify three additional types of health checks that the tasks should undergo: command-based, HTTP, and TCP.

Example 3-12 shows the common fields of the JSON health check specification.

Example 3-12. Common health check fields

```
{
    "gracePeriodSeconds": 300, ❶
    "intervalSeconds": 60, ❷
    "maxConsecutiveFailures": 3, ❸
    "timeoutSeconds": 30 ❹
}
```

❶ The grace period is the amount of time that a task is given to start itself up. Health checks will not begin to run against a particular task until this many seconds have elapsed. This parameter is optional, with a default value of a 5-minute grace period.

❷ The interval is the amount of time between runs of this health check. This parameter is optional, with a default value of 1 minute between each check.

❸ The maximum number of consecutive failures determines how many failed health checks in a row should cause Marathon to forcibly kill the task, so that it can be restarted elsewhere. If this is set to 0, then this health check failing will never result in the task getting killed. This parameter is optional, with tasks by default being killed after three failures of this health check.

❹ Sometimes, a health check just hangs. Rather than simply ignoring the check, Marathon will treat the slow or hung health check as a failure if it doesn't complete in this many seconds. This parameter is optional, and by default health checks have 20 seconds to run.

We'll look at the two of the three types of health checks here: HTTP and TCP. Command health checks are still relatively new, and due to some of their limitations, I recommend waiting a bit longer for them to stabilize. Bear in mind, though, that HTTP and TCP health checks here are currently performed by the Marathon master, which means that they're not scalable to thousands of tasks.[3]

HTTP checks

HTTP health checks validate if doing a GET on a particular route results in a successful HTTP status code. Successful status codes can either be true successes, or redirects; thus, the response code must be in the range 200–399, inclusive. To configure an HTTP health check, there are two required fields and one optional field, as shown in Example 3-13.

Example 3-13. HTTP health check fields

```
{
    "protocol": "HTTP", ❶
    "path": "/healthcheck", ❷
    "portIndex": 0 ❸
}
```

❶ You must specify that this is an HTTP health check in the "protocol" field.

❷ You must specify what the route for the health check should be. In this case, we're going to attempt a GET on http://myserver.example.com:8888/healthcheck, where myserver.example.com:8888 is the host and port that Marathon started the task on.

---

3 These will be made horizontally scalable in a future version of Mesos. You can see whether these features have been added yet by checking MESOS-2533 and MESOS-3567 on *https://issues.apache.org/jira*.

❸ You can optionally specify a `"portIndex"` for the health check. By default, the port index is 0.

Why Do Health Checks Use "portIndex" Instead of "port"?

You might be confused as to what the `"portIndex"` is in the health check specification, and why we don't simply specify the actual port. Remember that Marathon can (and by best practices does) choose the ports that your application will bind to. As a result, we don't actually know when we're configuring the health check what port the application is running on. Instead, however, remember that all the ports our application used were specified in the `"ports"` array of the application descriptor. Therefore, we can simply specify which index of the `"ports"` array corresponds to the port that we want to run the health check on!

TCP checks

TCP health checks validate whether it's possible to successfully open a TCP connection to the task. They do not send or receive any data—they simply attempt to open the socket. To configure a TCP health check, there is one required and one optional field, shown in Example 3-14.

Example 3-14. TCP health check fields

```
{
    "protocol": "TCP", ❶
    "portIndex": 0 ❷
}
```

❶ You must specify that this is a TCP health check in the `"protocol"` field.

❷ You can optionally specify a `"portIndex"` for the health check. By default, the port index is 0.

Application Versioning and Rolling Upgrades

What use would a distributed, scalable PaaS have if it couldn't do rolling upgrades? An *upgrade* is any time that you modify the application, which is typically done by making a PUT to the /v2/apps/$appid route on Marathon. Every upgrade creates a new version, which is named with the timestamp of when the upgrade was made. When you query the REST API for information about the application, every task will say which version it is running. You can query which versions are available from the /v2/apps/$appid/versions route on Marathon, and you can find details of the versions from the /v2/apps/$appid/versions/$version route. Example 3-15 demonstrates how to configure the upgrade behavior of an application.

Example 3-15. Application upgrades

```
{
    "upgradeStrategy": {
        "minimumHealthCapacity": 0.5,
        "maximumOverCapacity": 0.1
    }
}
```

With Marathon, you can easily specify how much of the application you want to be available during an upgrade via the "minimumHealthCapacity" field of the application descriptor. The "minimumHealthCapacity" can be set to any value between 0 and 1.

If you set this to 0, when you deploy a new version Marathon will first kill all the old tasks, then start up new ones.

If you set this to 0.6, when you deploy a new version Marathon will first kill 40% of the old tasks, then start up 60% of the new tasks, then kill the rest of the old tasks and start the rest of the new tasks.

If you set this to 1, when you deploy a new version Marathon will first start up all the new tasks (at which point your application could use twice as many resources as during regular operations), and then shut down the old tasks.

The "maximumOverCapacity" setting provides an additional level of safety, so that an application doesn't consume too many resources temporarily during an upgrade. The "maximumOverCapacity" can be set to any value between 0 and 1.

If you set this to 0, when you deploy a new version Marathon will not start more tasks than the target number of instances.

If you set this to 0.6, when you deploy a new version Marathon will never exceed a combined total of 160% of the target number of tasks.

If you set this to 1, when you deploy a new version Marathon will be allowed to start every new task before it kills any of the old tasks, if it so chooses.

The Event Bus

Often, when building applications with Marathon, you'll want to receive notifications when various events happen, such as when an application gets a new deployment, or when it scales up or down. These notifications could then be used to reconfigure proxies and routers, log statistics, and generate reports. Marathon has a built-in feature for automatically POSTing all of its internal events to a provided URI. To use this feature, simply provide two additional command-line arguments to Marathon:

--event_subscriber
> This argument should be passed the value http_callback in order to enable this subsystem. At this time, no other options are supported.

--http_endpoints
> This argument is a comma-separated list of destination URIs to send the JSON-formatted events to. For example, a valid argument would be http://host1/foo,http://host2/bar.

Setting Up HAProxy with Marathon

What a great day! We've learned all about Marathon and decided that it would make an excellent platform for our applications. Now that our applications are running on Marathon, however, we've reached an impasse: how can the outside world actually connect to them? Some types of applications, such as Celery or Resque workers, need no additional configuration: they communicate via a shared database. Other types of applications, such as HTTP servers and Redis instances, need to be made easily discoverable. The most popular way to do this on Mesos clusters is to run proxies on static, non-Mesos managed hosts, and automatically update those proxies to point at running instances of the application. This way, the application is always available on a known host and port (i.e., the proxy), but we can still dynamically scale its capacity on the backend. Also, each proxy host can typically serve many applications, each on a different port, so that a small number of proxy hosts are sufficient for hundreds of backends. Typically, proxies are constrained either by the total bandwidth used by all active connections, or by the total CPU usage if they're providing SSL termination.[4]

There are two proxies that are far and away the most popular choices for use in modern application stacks: HAProxy and Nginx. HAProxy is a proxy with very few features: it can proxy HTTP and TCP connections, perform basic health checks, and terminate SSL. It is built for stability and performance: there have been no reported crashes or deadlock bugs in HAProxy for 13 years. This is why HAProxy is popular amongst Mesos users today.

Nginx, by comparison, has no limits on its features. Besides acting as a proxy, it is able to run custom user code written in Lua, JavaScript, or JVM-based languages. This code can affect the proxy operations, or even serve responses directly. Many systems actually use both proxies: clients connect to HAProxy instances, which them-

---

4 SSL termination is when clients communicate with the proxy over a secure SSL connection, and the proxy handles the SSL so that the backends need not waste CPU resources on cryptography, or even support it.

selves forward the requests to Nginx instances. The Nginx instances then either respond directly, or proxy the requests to backend servers to be processed.

In this section, we're only going to discuss HAProxy, but be aware that Nginx can be used in exactly the same way, if you require the additional functionality it offers.

haproxy-marathon-bridge

In the Marathon repository, there's a script called *bin/haproxy-marathon-bridge*. This script is intended to help generate an HAProxy configuration file for Marathon. Unfortunately, it doesn't allow you to specify which port the services on Marathon will be bound to on the HAProxy host. As a result, this script is best avoided.

Let's take a look at the most popular configurations for setting up proxies with Mesos.

Bamboo

Bamboo (*https://github.com/QubitProducts/bamboo*) is an HAProxy configuration daemon with a web interface. It provides a UI for viewing and managing the current state of HAProxy rules. At its core, Bamboo monitors Marathon for changes to applications, and keeps its HAProxy instance's backends up-to-date. Bamboo also provides several useful features, all of which are exposed via the web interface and an HTTP REST API.

Most importantly, Bamboo supports using HAProxy ACL rules for each Marathon application. An ACL rule is a fine-grained way to choose which server backend should handle a request. ACL rules can route requests based on their URL, cookies, headers, and many other factors. For instance, you can use ACL rules to route requests whose paths start with `/static` to the static content-serving backends, but all other requests to your application servers. ACL rules are extremely powerful, since they allow you to separate your application into isolated components or services, scale those components separately, but still expose a single URL to clients. With ACL rules, you could choose to route anonymous visitors to one pool of servers, logged-in users to another pool of servers, and requests for static data to a third pool of servers, thus enabling you to scale each of their capacities separately.

Bamboo also has a powerful templating system, based on the Go language's `text/template` package (*http://golang.org/pkg/text/template/*). This templating system is flexible, but does have a steep learning curve compared to simpler, more popular systems like mustache templates (*https://mustache.github.io*).

All proxy configuration information is stored in ZooKeeper, which simplifies configuration management by keeping all instances of Bamboo in sync.

Bamboo uses the Marathon event bus to discover changes in backend configurations, which means that your HAProxy configurations typically lag changes in Marathon by mere hundreds of milliseconds.

Additionally, Bamboo has basic integration with StatsD (*https://github.com/etsy/statsd*) to report on when reconfiguration events occurred.

Bamboo provides a complete solution for sophisticated HAProxy configurations for Marathon applications.

HAProxy for microservices

Nowadays, microservices are a popular architectural pattern. Mesos and Marathon form a great substrate for building microservices-based applications: after all, you can host all your services on Marathon. Unfortunately, service discovery is typically a substantial problem for microservice deployments. Let's look at how we can use Mesos and Marathon to create a SmartStack (*http://nerds.airbnb.com/smartstack-service-discovery-cloud/*)-like system.

We need to consider two issues: how can we do service discovery, and what are the problems with the standard options? These options include:

DNS

We could choose to use round-robin DNS to give all our backend servers the same DNS name. There are two problems we'll face, however: DNS changes typically take at least several seconds to propagate through our infrastructure, and some applications cache DNS resolutions forever (meaning they'll never see DNS changes). The other problem is that, unless you write a custom client library that can use SRV records, DNS doesn't provided a simple solution to running multiple applications on the same server but with different or randomly assigned ports.

Centralized load balancing

This is akin to what we discussed in "Bamboo" on page 48. For some applications, this is actually a great design; however, it does require a globally accessible pool of load balancers. This centralization can make it tedious to securely isolate applications from one another: in order to isolate the applications, you must configure the Nginx or HAProxy rules for the specific isolation requirements.[5]

In-app discovery

Companies like Twitter and Google use specialized service request and discovery layers, such as Finagle and Stubby, respectively. These RPC layers integrate ser-

---

5 The other options, DNS and in-app discovery, delegate communication directly to each application, so there's no central system to configure for isolation. Instead, each application can handle its authorization in complete isolation from other applications.

vice discovery directly into the application, querying ZooKeeper or Chubby (Google's internal ZooKeeper-like system) when they need to find a server to which they can send a request. If this is possible in your environment, using a specialized service discovery layer offers the most flexibility in terms of routing, load balancing, and reliability due to the fact that you can control every aspect of the system. Unfortunately, if you need to integrate applications written in several languages, it can be onerous and time-consuming to develop parallel implementations of the discovery system for every language. Furthermore, this approach can be a nonstarter if you need to integrate with existing applications that weren't developed with this service discovery mechanism built in.

The shortcomings of these approaches led many engineers to come up with a fourth pattern: one that combines the ease of integration of centralized load balancing with the fault tolerance of the decentralized options. With this approach, we will run a copy of HAProxy on every single machine in our data center. Then, we'll assign each application a port (but not a hostname). Finally, we'll keep all of our HAProxy instances pointing each application's port at its backends, wherever they're running on the cluster.

This approach has two main benefits:

Ease of setup
> You can use Bamboo or a simple cron job on every machine in your cluster to keep the local instances of HAProxy in sync with Marathon. Even if some part of your infrastructure is temporarily unavailable, the local HAProxy will continue to route traffic directly to the backends. This means that even a disruption of Marthon won't impact the application's operations.

Ease of use
> Every application can communicate with any other microservice simply by connecting to localhost:$PORT, where $PORT is what you assigned to that microservice. There's no need to write any specialized or custom code for your applications, as all you need to do is remember which port corresponds to which application.

There are also a few downsides to this approach. One is that you need to carefully maintain the mapping from service to port. If you try to store that mapping globally and have applications fetch it on startup, you'll have to write custom code for every language again. On the other hand, if you hardcode the ports themselves, you run the risk of typos, which can be very difficult to debug.

The other downside is the lack of coordination between proxies. Our system continues to function even when partial failures happen, because each machine operates independently. Due to the independent operation of each machine, it's possible for several HAProxies to all route to the same backend, thus spiking the load on that backend, which can result in cascading failures. It is normal to see the variance of request times increase as the number of nodes in a cluster increases.

Today, this approach of tying services to ports and having every client connect to HAProxy at localhost seems to be the most popular way to manage service discovery on Mesos clusters.

Running Mesos Frameworks on Marathon

A very common choice in Mesos clusters is to run the cluster's Mesos frameworks on Marathon. But Marathon is a Mesos framework itself! So what does it mean to run a Mesos framework on Marathon? Rather than worrying about deploying each framework's scheduler to specific hosts and dealing with those hosts' failures, Marathon will ensure that the framework's scheduler is always running somewhere on the cluster. This greatly simplifies deploying new frameworks in a highly reliable configuration.

What About Resource Allocation for Frameworks Run by Marathon?

New Mesos users often wonder, "If I run a framework on Marathon, how does that affect the allocation of resources?" In fact, although the framework's scheduler is run by Marathon, the scheduler still must connect directly to Mesos, and *it will receive resources in an identical way as if you ran it on specifically chosen machines.* The benefit of running it on Marathon, of course, is that any Mesos slave can run the scheduler, and Marathon can restart it automatically if that slave fails.

What Is Chronos?

Chronos is a Mesos framework that provides a highly available, distributed time-based job scheduler, like cron. With Chronos, you can launch jobs that are either command-line programs (optionally downloaded from URIs) or Docker containers. Like Marathon, Chronos has a web UI and an easily programmable REST API. Although the Chronos endpoints have a slightly different interface than Marathon's, we won't go over their details, as the online documentation (*https://mesos.github.io/chronos/*) is sufficient. Chronos has four key features for scheduling jobs:

Interval scheduling
> Chronos uses the standard ISO 8601 notation to specify repeating intervals. Through the web UI or REST API, you can specify the frequency at which you want the job to rerun. This makes Chronos suitable for running quick jobs every few minutes, or a nightly data generation job.

Dependency tracking

In theory, Chronos supports dependent jobs. Dependent jobs run only if their prerequisites ran successfully. Unfortunately, Chronos's implementation of dependent jobs misses the mark. In Chronos, a job's dependencies are considered satisfied if the last invocation of that job was successful. A dependent job is run as soon as all of its dependencies have been run at least once. This means that unless every parent has the exact same interval, the dependent jobs can run at potentially unexpected times. In "Chronos Operational Concerns" on page 54, we'll look at a popular mitigation strategy for this.

Deferred start

Chronos can also be used to run a job once or on a repeating interval at a point in the future. When you specify the ISO 8601 interval on which to repeat the job, you also specify when you'd like the first run of the job to start. This means that you can use Chronos to schedule jobs to run days, weeks, or months in the future, which can be useful for planning purposes.

Worker scalability

The key differentiator between Chronos and most other job schedulers is that Chronos runs its jobs inside of containers on Mesos. This means that jobs are isolated and workers are scalable, so no matter what load Chronos generates, you're able to add new Mesos slaves to handle the additional work and ensure that the jobs receive their necessary resources.

Like all production-ready Mesos frameworks, Chronos has high-availability support with hot spares—most Chronos deployments will run at least two instances of the scheduler, to ensure that Chronos never has more than a couple seconds of downtime if a scheduler or its host fails. Chronos also comes with a synchronization tool, `chronos-sync.rb`. This tool synchronizes the Chronos state to disk in JSON format. Using `chronos-sync.rb`, you can version the jobs you run on your cluster by committing the file to version control. This is the most popular approach to ensure repeatability, since it allows you to keep your Chronos configuration in a repository.

The combination of its REST API and synchronize-to-disk tool make Chronos easy to integrate. Since its features are somewhat limited, it's easy to use, but it's not a complete solution for dependent workflow management.

Running Chronos on Marathon

One of the most common techniques seen in Mesos framework deployment is to run framework schedulers on Marathon. The reason for this is that those schedulers can rely on Marathon to ensure they're always running somewhere. This removes a huge burden from the operator, who would otherwise need to ensure that every scheduler had a well-monitored, multimachine deployment.

In order to be deployable on Marathon, a scheduler must do some sort of leader election. As we'll learn in Chapter 4, a scheduler connects to Mesos from a single host. This means that if we'd like to run our scheduler in two locations (e.g., to have a hot spare), we'll need some sort of signaling to ensure that only one scheduler runs at a time. The most common way to solve this is to use ZooKeeper, since it has an easily integrated leader election component (see "Adding High Availability" on page 79 for details). Marathon and Chronos both take this approach.

Let's look at an example JSON expression for launching Chronos on Marathon (Example 3-16). In order to maximize the efficiency of our port allocations, we'll allow Chronos to bind to any port. To connect to Chronos, we'll either click through the Marathon UI or use one of the HAProxy service discovery mechanisms described earlier.

Example 3-16. Chronos JSON descriptor

```
{
    "cmd": "java -jar chronos.jar -Xmx350m -Xms350m ---port $PORT0", ❶
    "uris": [
        "http://fetchable/uri/with/chronos.jar" ❷
    ],
    "cpus": 1, ❸
    "mem": 384, ❸
    "instances": 2, ❹
    "id": "chronos",
    "ports": [0], ❺
    "constraints": [["hostname", "UNIQUE"]] ❻
}
```

❶ We assume that `java` is already installed on all the Mesos slaves. Thus, we only need to pass the dynamically assigned port to Chronos so that it can start up successfully.

❷ Rather than installing Chronos on every Mesos slave, we'll store its *.jar* file in some known location. This way, it'll be downloaded on the fly to any slave that is assigned to run the Chronos scheduler, simplifying deployment.

❸ We'll choose a container size to match the amount of memory we allow the JVM to allocate (we leave 34 MB of headroom for the JVM itself).

❹ Running two instances of Chronos gives us near-instantaneous failover, since the standby Chronos scheduler will already be running.

❺ Chronos needs only one port to be assigned.

❻ We will use a unique host constraint to ensure that the standby instance of Chronos is running on a different machine. If there are slave attributes that indicate the rack of each slave, it would be better to rack-isolate the scheduler and its standby.

The simplest way to verify that Chronos is running is to click on the assigned port number from the Marathon app view. Each task's port assignment will be a link to that host and port combination, which will load the Chronos UI. The Chronos UI is somewhat buggy, so it's recommended to use `curl` or `chronos-sync.rb` to configure your instance of Chronos.

Chronos Operational Concerns

Chronos is a useful part of the Mesos ecosystem; however, care must be taken not to overly rely on it. There are a few things that one must be aware of when running Chronos in production:

1. The dependent jobs feature isn't useful—you must use a workflow manager.
2. Chronos is still a complex distributed system—it's only necessary if you need jobs to run scalably in containers.

Almost no one uses the Chronos dependent jobs feature. Instead, they use Chronos to schedule invocations of popular data workflow tools. For simple workflows (such as running a few processes in order), Bash scripts are a popular option; however, beyond 20 lines, Bash scripts become unwieldy, and their syntax for complex loops and conditionals leaves much to be desired. `make` is another popular way to express dependencies, since it has superior syntax for workflows and supports basic parallelism. Luigi (*https://github.com/spotify/luigi*) is a much richer and more powerful workflow manager. It supports checkpoints in HDFS and databases, which can improve the efficiency of retries of jobs that failed partway through, since it won't need to redo earlier checkpointed work. Regardless of your particular needs and use case, you should use some other tool to order the jobs that Chronos will be scheduling.

If you've made it this far, you're almost ready to use Chronos in production! The final consideration is whether you truly need the scalable isolation that Chronos gets from Mesos. Even though you're running a Mesos cluster, you don't need to use Chronos for your task management. There are many other job-scheduling servers that could easily be run on Marathon; only use Chronos if you need each job to run in its own container.

Chronos on Marathon: Summary

Chronos is a powerful tool for Mesos clusters that need reliable, scalable, interval-based job scheduling. It powers the data generation processes at many companies, including Airbnb. Just remember the several quirks, workarounds, and advice discussed here!

Chronos on Marathon is just one example of how Marathon can be used to provide high availability and ease of deployment to other Mesos schedulers. DCOS (*https://mesosphere.com/product/*), a commercial Mesos product, takes this further and requires all frameworks on DCOS to be hosted by Marathon. Whether you're deploying Chronos (*http://mesos.github.io/chronos/*), Kafka (*https://github.com/mesos/kafka*), or Cotton (*https://github.com/apache/incubator-cotton*), Marathon is an excellent choice for hosting other Mesos frameworks' schedulers.

Alternatives to Marathon + Chronos

Of course, Marathon (and Chronos) won't fit every cluster's needs. Let's briefly look at two other popular Mesos PaaS frameworks: Aurora and Singularity. Both frameworks have a much steeper learning curve, but they offer many additional features.

Singularity

Singularity (*https://github.com/HubSpot/Singularity*) is a Mesos framework developed by HubSpot. It offers the ability to deploy services just like Marathon (including Dockerized applications); beyond this, if a service begins to fail its health checks after a deployment, Singularity will automatically roll back the deployment. Singularity also supports repeating jobs, like Chronos, as well as one-shot jobs, which can be triggered via a REST API. This simplifies adding containerized, asynchronous background processing to any service or repeating job. For managing service discovery and proxies, Singularity is integrated with another tool called Baragon (*https://github.com/HubSpot/Baragon*), which manages and integrates HAProxy, Nginx, and Amazon's Elastic Load Balancer.

Aurora

Aurora (*http://aurora.apache.org/*) is the Mesos framework that powers Twitter. Aurora has a highly advanced job description API written in Python. This API, called Thermos, allows users to specify how to build and install applications, as well as the workflow and sequence of processes to run within the Mesos executor. Aurora comes with a high-performance distributed service discovery API with bindings for C++, Java, and Python. It's able to run repeating jobs with cron-style syntax. Also, just like Singularity, Aurora can automatically detect when a service's health checks start failing and roll it back to the previous working version. Aurora's most powerful features are related to its multitenancy controls: Aurora can allow for some tasks to use spare cluster capacity, and then preempt those tasks when higher-priority production tasks need to be scheduled. It also can enforce quotas between users. These features were born out of the needs of a company running huge numbers of applications written by hundreds of developers on massive Mesos clusters; if that sounds like the kind of organization you're building a Mesos cluster for, Aurora's worth a closer look.

Summary

In this chapter, we learned how to build standard stateless server-based applications with Mesos. What we achieved was self-healing, self-restarting, and simplified service discovery—we basically built a PaaS on Mesos! This was accomplished by using Marathon, a popular Mesos framework.

Marathon launches, monitors, and restarts processes across your Mesos cluster. It simplifies rollout, allows for push-button scale up and scale down, and provides a simple JSON API that's easy to integrate with.

First, we learned how to start up Marathon, how to secure it, and how to ensure that it's highly available. Then, we learned how to write a Marathon service descriptor, which allowed us to launch the omnipresent SimpleHTTPServer. This was just an example application; any other application could be launched simply by changing the command line. We also learned how to programmatically query for information about the status of applications on Marathon.

Next, we learned about scaling applications on Marathon. Most importantly, we discussed placement constraints, and how to easily ensure that applications run on the correct class of slave machines and are spread evenly amongst racks.

Docker is the most popular application containerization technology. We learned how to launch Dockerized applications on Marathon with minimal fuss, and how to configure various Docker-specific options, such as mounting host disks.

Our applications wouldn't be fully robust without including health checks and automatic incremental rollouts and rollbacks. We discussed how to configure TCP, HTTP, and command-based health checks, as well as how to specify the application's behavior during upgrades. We also discussed how to subscribe to an event stream from Marathon to build custom integrations.

Then, we learned about integrating Marathon with a service discovery proxy. Bamboo, an open-source HAProxy configuration manager, is a powerful tool for synchronizing HAProxy with Marathon tasks. We also learned about popular approaches for building scalable, multilanguage microservices architectures with HAProxy and Marathon.

Finally, we looked at how to use Marathon to host other Mesos frameworks' schedulers, using Chronos, a distributed cron-like framework, as an example. We also briefly surveyed alternative PaaS frameworks to Marathon, since they offer many additional features (at the cost of a steeper learning curve).

Perhaps Marathon and its alternatives don't satisfy the needs of your application, and you need more control over how processes are launched or how failures are handled. In that case, you'll need to write your own framework. In the next chapter, we'll learn about the techniques used to build Marathon, so that you can build your own custom Mesos framework.

CHAPTER 4

Creating a New Framework for Mesos

A Mesos framework is the conceptual aggregation of a distributed system. But what does that mean to us, as framework developers? How can we actually understand how the structure of the code we write maps onto the Mesos cluster? Let's review the Mesos architecture, and learn some common patterns in framework design.

Instead of trying to understand everything about Mesos architecture all at once, we'll look at the simplest case: a framework that only has a scheduler, and no custom executor. This type of framework could spin up workers to process requests coming in on a queue, or it could manage a pool of services.

The Scheduler

The scheduler is the component that interacts directly with the leading Mesos master. A scheduler has four responsibilities:

1. Launch tasks on the received offers.
2. Handle status updates from those tasks, particularly to respond to task failures and crashes.
3. Persist state and manage failovers in order to be highly available.
4. Interact with clients, users, or other systems (since no system runs in a vacuum!).

Some of these responsibilities are implemented purely by interacting with the Mesos API; others must be implemented using the language of choice's platform. For instance, launching tasks and handling status updates are implemented entirely by Mesos callbacks and API requests. On the other hand, it's up to you to start a web server (such as Jetty on Java or Flask on Python) to allow clients to interact with the scheduler. High availability usually requires using both Mesos APIs and other libraries to create a solution that is suitable for the problem domain.

But how can we launch tasks if we're only focusing on the scheduler? For our convenience, Mesos comes with something called the CommandExecutor, which is specifically designed to make it easy to launch and orchestrate command-line programs and Docker containers. Let's take a look at some high-level designs for several common scheduler abstractions: building a pool of servers, a work queue, and a job processor.

First, we'll look at the pool of servers design. Its architecture is illustrated in Figure 4-1.

Pool of Servers Scheduler

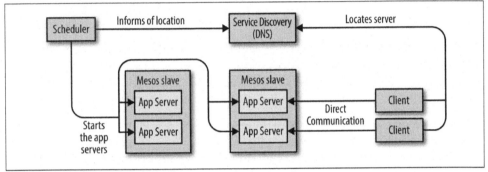

Figure 4-1. Architecture and information flow of a pool of servers scheduler

This scheduler is simply going to ensure that there are always X copies of some application, such as Ruby on Rails, running. To build a pool of servers, our scheduler will have a list of all the servers it wants to be running. Initially, the list will have all the servers in the *pending* state. As the scheduler receives offers, it will attempt to launch servers, putting them into the *staging* state. Once the servers start successfully, the scheduler can move them to the *running* state. If they ever crash, they'll go back to the initial pending state so that they can be relaunched on a new offer. Note that we need three states here: pending, staging, and running.

You might be tempted to remove the staging state, since, after all, that seems awfully similar to pending—in both cases, the server is not yet started. But here's the problem: Mesos is an asynchronous system! You could receive many offers between attempting to launch a task and having the task actually start. Thus, the staging state ensures that we only try to launch each server once, and only retry if the launch fails. If you forget to have a staging state, you might encounter a bug in which there are tens or hundreds of instances of a task when there should be only one.

Work Queue Scheduler

The work queue architecture, illustrated in Figure 4-2, allows clients to submit "work items" to a queue, where they'll eventually be processed by workers. A work queue scheduler will ensure that we always have a sufficient number of workers running, so that there will be a sufficient number of workers to process the queued work items.

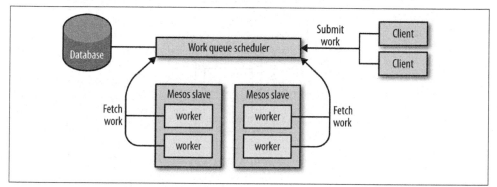

Figure 4-2. Architecture and information flow of a work queue scheduler

To build this scheduler, we're actually going to cheat and assume that we already have a pool of servers scheduler, as described in the previous section. This way, we simply start the workers as servers in the pool. Therefore, the meat of this system will reside in the workers themselves.

Our workers will retrieve their work items from some known location. This location could be passed to them from the scheduler as a command-line option or environment variable. Each worker will connect to the queue, and then loop forever: retrieve an item, process it, and mark it as done.

The neat thing about considering work queues (and all potential frameworks) in this way is that you don't even need to write a scheduler—you could just use Marathon or some other pool of services scheduler. Of course, this shifts the implementation of the queue to another system, such as RabbitMQ or Redis. This is a good thing: the Mesos messaging APIs are designed for controlling the applications on the cluster and are not as well suited to other domains, such as transactional logic or high-performance messaging. When developing frameworks for Mesos, you must use appropriate data storage backends—queues, databases, and document stores are all likely useful, depending on the framework you're building.

Job Processor Scheduler

The final abstraction we'll consider is the job processor scheduler (Figure 4-3).

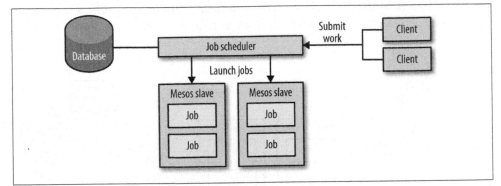

Figure 4-3. Architecture and information flow of a job processor scheduler

A job processor will accept a list of jobs from clients and then run those jobs on a cluster; a job is just a command line to invoke, along with the CPU and memory resources it needs. This scheduler will require a slightly more complex state machine, since we'll also need terminal states for jobs (we'll call them *successful* and *failed*). We'll also track how many retries have been attempted, so that we can give up on jobs with no hope for success.

This scheduler's state machine will move jobs from pending to staging when it attempts to launch them on an offer, and from staging to running when the job actually starts running. Handling completion of a task is trickier, though: we'll want to move the job to successful if it succeeds, to failed if it has exceeded the maximum number of retries, or to pending if it has more retries remaining. Furthermore, we could determine whether the task failed due to a bug in its code, a transient machine failure, or some other issue—this is useful feedback for deciding whether to have the job fail fast, or let it continue to retry.

Now that we've seen conceptually how a framework could be implemented with just a scheduler, let's try our hand at implementing the job processor.

Useless Remote BASH

Before we get started on the job processor, let's break down the absolute minimal code needed to get a task to launch on Mesos. We'll call this program Useless Remote BASH,[1] as it'll just run the hardcoded program in a container on the cluster.

Let's break down this most simple of frameworks into several parts, and see why each part is necessary. In Example 4-1, we can see the imports and class declaration of our new scheduler.

Example 4-1. Imports and class declaration of useless remote BASH

```
package com.example;
import java.nio.file.*;
import java.util.*;
import org.apache.mesos.*;
import org.apache.mesos.Protos.*;

public class UselessRemoteBASH implements Scheduler {
    // We'll discuss the inner bits as we go
}
```

Two things here deserve our attention:

1. We import everything from `org.apache.mesos` and `org.apache.mesos.Protos`, so that we can use the Mesos APIs.

2. Schedulers should implement the `Scheduler` interface, which defines the messages a scheduler can receive as callbacks.

We'll use the complementary `SchedulerDriver` class to send messages to Mesos. Example 4-2 is the entry point of our program.

Example 4-2. main of Useless Remote BASH

```
public static void main(String ... args) throws Exception {
    FrameworkInfo frameworkInfo = FrameworkInfo.newBuilder()
        .setUser("")
        .setName("Useless Remote BASH")
        .build();

    Scheduler mySched = new UselessRemoteBASH();
```

---

1 The name of this framework refers to it hardcoding the command that it runs; as an example of how to work with the Mesos APIs, it is very useful.

```
SchedulerDriver driver = new MesosSchedulerDriver(
    mySched,
    frameworkInfo,
    "zk://" + args[0] + "/mesos"
);
driver.start();
driver.join();
}
```

In the `main` function, first, we construct the `FrameworkInfo` of our framework. `FrameworkInfo` is a protobuf that describes the framework to Mesos. You'll want to choose a clear name for the framework, so that you can identify your framework in the Mesos UI. In practice, you'll want to construct the name to include several pieces of data: which framework this is, as well as other high-level information about the framework, such as whether it's a `dev` or `prod` instance. It's entirely up to you what you name your framework, but consider the anecdote in the following sidebar!

When Poorly Chosen Framework Names Become Annoying

We decided it'd be effective to run Spark on our Mesos cluster. We also decided that every user would get their own instance of Spark. The next day, a user complained that tasks weren't getting scheduled. We opened the Mesos UI to see what was happening, but to our chagrin, every single user's Spark framework was just called `Spark 0.7.6`. As a result, we had no way to identify which user was hogging the resources! From then on, we made sure to change the name of the Spark framework to `$username Spark 0.7.6`, so that we could tell what our cluster was doing at a glance.

Typically, we set the framework's user to an empty string (`""`), which means that it will register with Mesos as whichever user is running the scheduler. In "Roles" on page 17, we discussed how the framework's user can be used for quotas, capacity planning, and security. Most of the other fields of `FrameworkInfo` are used to configure high availability, so we'll postpone discussing those until later.

After we've constructed our `FrameworkInfo`, we can create the *driver*, which is the component that actually communicates with Mesos. The driver for the scheduler is an instance of `SchedulerDriver`; you should stick with the `MesosSchedulerDriver` that is built with Mesos for now. In the future, other implementations may be written in order to remove the dependencies on native code. Unfortunately, the current projects working on this are more trouble than they're worth for framework developers, as

---

they haven't reached stability yet.[2] The `SchedulerDriver` takes three arguments: an implementation of the Mesos `Scheduler` interface, the `FrameworkInfo`, and the address of the Mesos cluster. At this point, when we call `start()`, our driver will connect to the Mesos cluster, register the framework, and begin receiving offers. Usually, you'll want to call `join()` at the end of your `main` function. `join()` blocks until the driver terminates, either from having `stop()` called on it or because Mesos instructed the driver to stop because the framework failed over.

A Common Pattern for Starting the SchedulerDriver

Often, the last thing our main function does is call `start()` followed by `join()`. Because this is so common, you can just call `run()`, which is essentially `start() && join()`.

Now that we've seen how frameworks start up, let's look at Example 4-3. This function is an example of how to create a Mesos task that we can launch. As this is a useless framework, we hardcode what would normally be important parameters: the `cpus`, `mem`, and `command` we want to run.

Example 4-3. makeTask of Useless Remote BASH

```
public static TaskInfo makeTask(SlaveID targetSlave) {
    double cpus = 1.0;
    double mem = 100.0;
    String command = "echo hello world";

    UUID uuid = UUID.randomUUID();
    TaskID id = TaskID.newBuilder() ❶
        .setValue(uuid.toString())
        .build();
    return TaskInfo.newBuilder() ❷
        .setName("useless_remote_bash.task " + id.getValue())
        .setTaskId(id)
        .addResources(Resource.newBuilder() ❸
                .setName("cpus")
                .setType(Value.Type.SCALAR)
                .setScalar(Value.Scalar.newBuilder().setValue(cpus)))
        .addResources(Resource.newBuilder() ❸
                .setName("mem")
                .setType(Value.Type.SCALAR)
                .setScalar(Value.Scalar.newBuilder().setValue(mem)))
        .setCommand(CommandInfo.newBuilder().setValue(command)) ❹
```

---

2 Some projects to watch for purely native Mesos bindings are Jesos (*https://github.com/groupon/jesos*) for Java, Pesos (*https://github.com/wickman/pesos*) for Python, and Go bindings (*https://github.com/mesos/mesos-go*) for Go.

```
        .setSlaveId(targetSlave) ❺
        .build();
}
```

❶ First, we make a `TaskID`. The `TaskID` must be unique to the framework, just as the `ExecutorID` must be unique to the slave and the `SlaveID` must be unique to the cluster. I typically find it easiest to just use UUIDs appended to any IDs I need to generate, since that way I don't need to ever worry about the uniqueness constraints that Mesos requires.

❷ Next, we make the `TaskInfo`, which is the protobuf that explains how to launch a task. The `TaskInfo` requires you to set a name for the task. This name is what's displayed in the UI, and many Mesos tools can interact with it, such as the Mesos CLI. Typically, you'll want to set the name of the task to include useful specifying information, such as the framework name and any related entity (such as the app in Marathon or job in Hadoop). By writing the name from most general (i.e., framework) to most specific (i.e., instance of the task), you'll benefit from tools that can provide tab completion and autocompletion of the task names.

❸ A task wouldn't be useful without any resources: `TaskInfo` is where you can add all of the resources that the task will consume. The only two resources that you'll always want to specify are `cpus` and `mem` (note the s at the end of `cpus`); if your application listens to the network, you should also specify `ports`. There are many other resource types that Mesos can manage; you can read more about them in "Resources" on page 13.

❹ Since this framework is very simple, we set the command so that the Mesos `CommandExecutor` will handle the actual running of our task. We specify our command to the `CommandInfo` that we provide as the command; its features are discussed in "CommandInfo" on page 93. For the `CommandExecutor`, the `TaskID` and the `ExecutorID` are the same.

❺ Finally, we must tie this `TaskInfo` to the offer. Since it's possible to apply several offers from the same slave to one task (pooling them for more total resources), we specify the `SlaveID` of the slave we want the task to launch on rather than the `OfferID`s that we want it to use. When we actually call `launchTasks()`, that's where we'll link the offers to the `TaskInfo` (see the note Combining Offers following Example 4-5).

We've managed to register our framework, and we've learned how to specify a task to launch. The last step is to actually implement that pesky `Scheduler` interface. For this super-basic framework, we're going to ignore most of the callbacks, as they update us on information we don't want to react to. Note that all of the callbacks provide you with a driver; this driver is guaranteed to be the same one you called `start()` on. Mesos passes you this as a convenience, since it's the only way to interact with the cluster, and that's typically something you'd like to do in response to cluster events. Example 4-4 shows the callbacks we want to log: `registered` and `statusUpdate`.

Example 4-4. Scheduler callbacks to log

```
public void registered(SchedulerDriver driver, FrameworkID frameworkId,
                        MasterInfo masterInfo) {
    System.out.println("Registered with framework id " + frameworkId);
}

public void statusUpdate(SchedulerDriver driver, TaskStatus status) {
    System.out.println("Got status update "+status);
}
```

When we have successfully registered with the Mesos masters, we'll get the `registered` callback. When you register a framework for the first time, you don't specify the `FrameworkID`; instead, Mesos will assign it for you. This callback is the only place to learn the assignment of the `FrameworkID`. (In Example 4-15 and Example 4-14, we'll see how we can use this `FrameworkID` to safely fail a scheduler over to a new instance, so that we can build zero-downtime systems.) The `MasterInfo` tells you which port and version the master is running on. Frameworks can decide which Mesos features are valid to use based on the master's version.

The `statusUpdate` callback will soon become very important for our scheduler, as it's how we track the lifecycle of our tasks: when they start running, and when and why they fail. Even though we're not going to do anything with this callback yet, it's convenient to log when it happens, as that will help us debug our framework and confirm tasks that are actually launching and finishing. Whenever I build a production framework, I always make sure to enable logging for every `statusUpdate` callback: those logs have helped me identify and debug issues countless times.

Finally, we get to look at the core of our new framework, as shown in Example 4-5. This callback is how we receive offers from Mesos—offers that are chock-full of juicy resources that we can launch tasks on.

Example 4-5. Implementation of resourceOffers

```
private boolean submitted = false;

public void resourceOffers(SchedulerDriver driver, java.util.List<Offer> offers) {
    synchronized (this) {
        if (submitted) { ❶
            for (Offer o : offers) { ❷
                driver.declineOffer(o.getId());
```

```
        }
        return;
    }
    submitted = true;
    Offer offer = offers.get(0);
    TaskInfo ti = makeTask(offer.getSlaveId()); ❸
    driver.launchTasks( ❹
        Collections.singletonList(offer.getId()),
        Collections.singletonList(ti)
    );
    System.out.println("Launched offer: " + ti);
    }
}
```

❶   In our framework, we first check if we've already submitted our task.

❷   If we have, we simply decline all the offers.

❸   If we haven't submitted our task yet, we construct a `TaskInfo` for it with the ID of the slave from the first offer we received.

❹   Then, we call `launchTasks` to attempt to launch the task!

Combining Offers

`launchTasks` takes a list of offers, which allows us to combine several offers for the same slave in order to pool those offers' resources. It also takes a list of tasks, so that you can launch as many tasks as fit on the given offers. Note that all the tasks and offers must be for the same slave—the `launchTasks` will fail if they're not. If you want to launch tasks on multiple slaves, simply call `launchTasks` multiple times.

The other `Scheduler` callbacks, listed in Example 4-6, can all be ignored for now.

Example 4-6. Ignored callbacks for Useless Remote BASH

```
public void disconnected(SchedulerDriver driver) { }
public void error(SchedulerDriver driver, java.lang.String message) { }
public void executorLost(SchedulerDriver driver, ExecutorID executorId,
                        SlaveID slaveId, int status) { }
public void frameworkMessage(SchedulerDriver driver, ExecutorID executorId,
                            SlaveID slaveId, byte[] data) { }
public void offerRescinded(SchedulerDriver driver, OfferID offerId) { }
public void reregistered(SchedulerDriver driver, MasterInfo masterInfo) { }
public void slaveLost(SchedulerDriver driver, SlaveID slaveId) { }
```

And there you have it! You've written your first Mesos framework, and it actually does quite a lot. It can register with the master, create a `TaskInfo` to express how to launch a task, log status updates, and accept an offer to launch the task.

executorLost Doesn't Do Anything

Unfortunately, there's one scheduler callback that isn't actually implemented or supported by Mesos: `executorLost`. If you'd like to be notified about when an executor shuts down, we discuss a solution in "Canary tasks" on page 120. This issue is being pursued in MESOS-313 (*http://bit.ly/MESOS313*), so future versions of Mesos will implement this callback.

This Framework actually has two problematic bugs: when it accepts the offer to launch a task, it fails to check if the offer is actually big enough. If the offer was too small, we'll get a `TASK_LOST` status update about the task, rather than anything indicating success. The other bug is that when it accepts the offer, it doesn't decline the other offers that were potentially received in the `resourceOffers` callback. Those other offers will be stuck in a limbo state until they expire, which could be several minutes (or forever, if you didn't change the default). They'll be unavailable to other frameworks in the meantime.

In the coming sections, we'll improve `resourceOffers` to fix these issues.

Implementing a Basic Job Processor

Now, let's extend our framework to be more useful by reading a list of jobs from a JSON file, and then having it launch all of those jobs on Mesos. We'll start by looking at how we'll model a job (Example 4-7).

Example 4-7. Job implementation

```
public class Job {
    private double cpus; ❶
    private double mem; ❶
    private String command; ❶
    private boolean submitted; ❷

    private Job() {
        submitted = false;
    }

    public TaskInfo makeTask(SlaveID targetSlave) { ❸
        UUID uuid = UUID.randomUUID();
        TaskID id = TaskID.newBuilder()
            .setValue(uuid.toString())
```

```
        .build();
    return TaskInfo.newBuilder()
        .setName("task " + id.getValue())
        .setTaskId(id)
        .addResources(Resource.newBuilder()
                .setName("cpus")
                .setType(Value.Type.SCALAR)
                .setScalar(Value.Scalar.newBuilder().setValue(cpus)))
        .addResources(Resource.newBuilder()
                .setName("mem")
                .setType(Value.Type.SCALAR)
                .setScalar(Value.Scalar.newBuilder().setValue(mem)))
        .setSlaveId(targetSlave)
        .setCommand(CommandInfo.newBuilder().setValue(command))
        .build();
    }

    public static Job fromJSON(JSONObject obj) throws JSONException { ❹
        Job job = new Job();
        job.cpus = obj.getDouble("cpus");
        job.mem = obj.getDouble("mem");
        job.command = obj.getString("command");
        return job;
    }

    // ... snip ... ❺
}
```

❶ As you can see, we have parameterized the CPU, memory, and command arguments.

❷ We've moved the submitted field into the Job, so that we can track its lifecycle.

❸ We've moved the makeTask function into the Job as well, so that it can access all the local fields of the Job.

❹ For convenience, we've defined a single way to construct a Job, via the factory method fromJSON.

❺ I've left out the getter and setter definitions.

The Job is a container for information about a particular job, like a model class in MVC. We've only added two special methods: fromJSON, which gives us a way to construct the Job with valid starting state, and makeTask, which gives us a way to easily turn it into a TaskInfo without having all the protobuf munging code in our scheduler class.

Next, let's look at how our main function has evolved. Example 4-8 shows the revised version.

Example 4-8. Revised main for Useless Remote BASH

```java
public static void main(String ... args) throws Exception {
    byte[] data = Files.readAllBytes(Paths.get(args[1])); ❶
    JSONObject config = new JSONObject(new String(data, "UTF-8")); ❷
    JSONArray jobsArray = config.getJSONArray("jobs");
    List<Job> jobs = new ArrayList<>();
    for (int i = 0; i < jobsArray.length(); i++) { ❸
        jobs.add(Job.fromJSON(jobsArray.getJSONObject(i)));
    }

    System.out.println(jobs);

    // Below here, the function remains almost as before
    FrameworkInfo frameworkInfo = FrameworkInfo.newBuilder()
        .setUser("")
        .setName("Useless Remote BASH")
        .build();

    Scheduler mySched = new UselessRemoteBASH(jobs); ❹
    SchedulerDriver driver = new MesosSchedulerDriver(
        mySched,
        frameworkInfo,
        "zk://" + args[0] + "/mesos"
    );
    driver.start();
    driver.join();
}
```

❶ This allows us to read the entire contents of a file into memory. We assume that the first argument is still the Mesos cluster, and the second argument is the name of a file that contains the JSON configuration.

❷ We convert the byte array to JSON in this step, so that we can extract the Job configurations.

❸ Finally, we loop over the JSON job descriptors, processing them into Jobs.

❹ This time, we pass an argument to our Scheduler: the jobs we want it to launch.

Let's take a look at a sample JSON file of jobs, to get a feel for the schema:

```json
{
    "jobs": [ ❶
        {
            "cpus": 0.5, ❷
            "mem": 100,
            "command": "sleep 60; echo hello world"
        }
    ]
}
```

❶ The JSON file should contain a JSON object with a single key, jobs. That key's value should be a list of Job objects.

❷ Each job object has three properties: cpus, mem, and command, which correspond to the eponymous fields in the Job class.

Now that we can load jobs up, let's see how we evolved resourceOffers. The new version is shown in Example 4-9.

Example 4-9. Revised implementation of resourceOffers

```java
public void resourceOffers(SchedulerDriver driver, java.util.List<Offer> offers) {
    synchronized (jobs) {
        List<Job> pendingJobs = new ArrayList<>(); ❶
        for (Job j : jobs) { ❷
            if (!j.isSubmitted()) {
                pendingJobs.add(j);
            }
        }
        for (Offer o : offers) { ❸
            if (pendingJobs.isEmpty()) { ❹
                driver.declineOffer(o.getId());
                break;
            }
            Job j = pendingJobs.remove(0); ❺
            TaskInfo ti = j.makeTask(o.getSlaveId());
            driver.launchTasks(
                Collections.singletonList(o.getId()),
                Collections.singletonList(ti)
            );
            j.setSubmitted(true); ❻
        }
    }
}
```

❶ Because our Jobs contain state information (i.e., whether or not they were just launched), we need to first calculate which jobs haven't yet been launched.

❷ This loop allows us to find all the jobs that haven't been submitted yet, and add them to `pendingJobs`.

❸ Now, we're going to try to match jobs to offers.

❹ If we have no more jobs we want to launch, then we can decline the offer.

❺ If we reach this line, we have a job to launch. From here on, the code is similar to our first incarnation.

❻ Remember that we want to mark the job as submitted, or else we could accidentally double-submit the job.

This version of `resourceOffers` shows us several useful patterns. Every framework needs to keep track of the running tasks and work that it wants to do in the future. For most frameworks, it will be most convenient to have a single data structure that tracks all ongoing work. This data structure will include both running and pending tasks. Of course, when you actually want to launch a task, you'll need to calculate the specific set of tasks that are still pending. In this example, after each resource offer, we compute the set of pending tasks. Later in this chapter, we'll look at other architectures for tracking this information.

The other pattern that every framework uses is looping over all the offers, matching offers to pending work until one or the other is exhausted. But you might be thinking: `resourceOffers` requires a lot of care, and this framework still fails to handle it effectively! You'd be absolutely correct, which is why we're going to look at how to fix that problem now.

Matching Tasks to Offers

As we've been alluding to throughout this chapter, the assignment of tasks to offers is fraught with details that must be attended to. For instance, we must ensure that the offer has all the necessary resources for our job, we must attempt to launch as many tasks as we can on each offer, and we must prioritize which task we'll launch next. The reason we want to match as many tasks as possible to each offer is that if we only match one task per offer, our scheduler will launch tasks at a slow rate. Specifically:

$$\text{tasks launched per minute} = \frac{\text{number of slaves}}{\text{offer interval}}$$

With the default offer interval of 1 second, if you have a five-slave cluster, you'll only be able to launch at most 60 tasks per minute. With properly implemented offer handling code, however, you could launch tens of thousands of tasks per minute! For our example, we're going to implement the first fit algorithm, since it requires very little code. Then, we'll learn about other algorithms, and various considerations therein. Let's make the following change to our resourceOffers:

```
... // code unchanged
driver.launchTasks(
    Collections.singletonList(o.getId()),
    doFirstFit(o, pendingJobs);
);
... // code unchanged
```

Instead of directly taking a job, we're going to compute the first fit of all the pending jobs to the given offer. The solution we find is a List of tasks, since the whole point is that we can launch multiple tasks on a single offer.

doFirstFit's Semantics

doFirstFit takes an Offer and a list of Jobs and returns a list of TaskInfos that we can launch on the cluster. Note that doFirstFit is designed to remove all the Jobs that it decides to match from the list of Jobs passed into it.

Obviously, the interesting part is the implementation of doFirstFit (Example 4-10). The idea of first fit is this: given the amount of space available in an offer, we'll add tasks that fit in whatever space is left in the offer. When we decide to add a task, we'll deduct its space usage from the remaining space. Once we can't fit any more tasks into the offer, we'll remove all the matched Jobs from the list of Job provided as an argument, and we'll return the TaskInfos that will launch those Jobs.

Example 4-10. First-fit offer packing

```
public List<TaskInfo> doFirstFit(Offer offer, List<Job> jobs) {
    List<TaskInfo> toLaunch = new ArrayList<>();
    List<Job> launchedJobs = new ArrayList<>();
    double offerCpus = 0; ❶
    double offerMem = 0;
    // We always need to extract the resource info from the offer.
    // It's a bit annoying in every language.
    for (Resource r : offer.getResourcesList()) { ❷
        if (r.getName().equals("cpus")) {
            offerCpus += r.getScalar().getValue();
        } else if (r.getName().equals("mem")) {
            offerMem += r.getScalar().getValue();
        }
    }
    // Now, we will pack jobs into the offer
    for (Job j : jobs) {
        double jobCpus = j.getCpus();
```

```
        double jobMem = j.getMem();
        if (jobCpus <= offerCpus && jobMem <= offerMem) { ❸
            offerCpus -= jobCpus;
            offerMem -= jobMem;
            toLaunch.add(j.makeTask(offer.getSlaveId()));
            j.setSubmitted(true);
            launchedJobs.add(j); ❹
        }
    }
    for (Job j : launchedJobs) {
        j.launch(); ❺
    }
    jobs.removeAll(launchedJobs);
    return toLaunch;
}
```

❶ We'll keep track of how many resources are remaining in the offer in these variables.

❷ You must iterate over all the resources in the offer to find the ones whose names match the type of resource you care about, and only then can you extract the value. The reason this cannot be a map is that you can receive multiple resources of the same name; for example, you could receive both reserved and unreserved memory resources from a slave.

❸ Here, we check to see if the offer still has enough resources remaining to launch our task. If it does, we'll deduct those resources from our method's internal count, add the TaskInfo to the list of tasks we will launch, and mark the job as submitted.

❹ In order to support doFirstFit semantics, we add all jobs we'll launch to a list, so that we can remove all those elements from the original list of all pending jobs.

❺ Job has methods that help us track its instances' progress through their state machine. We'll go over this in Example 4-11.

First fit is usually the best algorithm to use when matching tasks to offers. You might think that this won't always utilize offers as efficiently as if you put more work into trying to optimize matching the offers. That's absolutely true, but consider the following: a cluster either has sufficient or insufficient resources for launching every pending task. If there are plenty of resources, then first fit should always be able to launch every task. If, on the other hand, there are not enough resources, nothing would be able to launch every task. Thus, it's a good idea to write code to choose which task to run next, so that you can maintain the target quality of service. Only if there are just barely enough resources does more sophisticated packing begin to make sense. Unfortunately for us, this problem—known more generally as the *knapsack problem*

—is a notorious NP-complete problem. NP-complete problems are those problems for which it can be proved that an optimal solution will take an extremely long time to find, and there's not a clever trick in existence to solve the problem faster.[3]

Actually, the situation isn't so bad. In fact, although it's impossible to solve the packing problem *perfectly* and quickly, there are several techniques that give "good enough" results and aren't too tricky to implement. For some frameworks, all tasks will be bottlenecked on a single resource: either CPUs (for compute-bound workloads, like data analysis) or memory (i.e., caches like memcached or Redis). As a result, when we try to pack our resources, we can simplify the packing problem to a single dimension: the most constrained dimension. Once we've done this, we can use techniques such as the fully polynomial time greedy approximation scheme for the 0/1 knapsack problem.[4]

Bridging the Semantic Gap Between Offers and Jobs

Now, we've got a pretty cool framework. It takes a JSON configuration file filled with the jobs we want to run, and it submits those jobs to the Mesos cluster efficiently. We have a problem, though—what if a job fails? At the moment, we'll just see a bit of output in the terminal indicating that the task failed, succeeded, or was lost. We want to add support for retries: when a job fails, we'll resubmit it in the hope that it will succeed this time. Eventually, however, we'll give up and consider it truly failed. To this end, we're going to expand our Job class so that instead of simply having a Boolean property submitted, it will have a JobState:

```
public enum JobState {
    PENDING,
    STAGING,
    RUNNING,
    SUCCESSFUL,
    FAILED
}
```

We need to increase the number of states a job can be in in order to support retries. Before, we would simply launch unsubmitted jobs. Now, we'll need to track the exact part of the task lifecycle a job is in, and resubmit it only if it has already failed. Figure 4-4 illustrates the valid state transitions.

---

[3] NP-completeness is out of scope for this book, but you can start with the Wikipedia article (*https://en.wikipedia.org/wiki/NP-complete*).

[4] This is also outside the scope of this book; for more information, see the Wikipedia page (*http://en.wikipedia.org/wiki/Knapsack_problem*) on the knapsack problem.

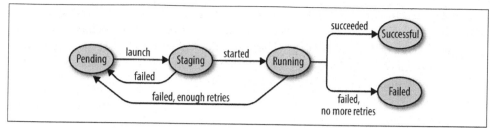

Figure 4-4. Valid transitions of JobState

We'll also have to expand the Job class to internally keep track of retries and the job's state. Example 4-11 shows the new methods that will implement the preceding state transition diagram.

Example 4-11. State transition methods for Job

```java
public class Job {
    // previous fields elided
    private int retries;

    private Job() {
        status = JobState.PENDING;
        id = UUID.randomUUID().toString();
        retries = 3;
    }

    public void launch() {
        status = JobState.STAGING;
    }

    public void started() {
        status = JobState.RUNNING;
    }

    public void succeed() {
        status = JobState.SUCCESSFUL;
    }

    public void fail() {
        if (retries == 0) {
            status = JobState.FAILED;
        } else {
            retries--;
            status = JobState.PENDING;
        }
    }
}
```

We've decided to give every job three retries. To simplify the implementation of the state changes of the job, we have four functions to move between states: launch(), started(), succeed(), and fail(). These functions will be called, respectively, when we submit the task to Mesos, when it starts, and when it succeeds or fails. Example 4-12 shows how we move between states.

Example 4-12. Enhanced statusUpdate handler

```
public void statusUpdate(SchedulerDriver driver, TaskStatus status) {
    synchronized (jobs) {
        // We'll see if we can find a job this corresponds to
        for (Job j : jobs) { ❶
            if (j.getId().equals(status.getTaskId().getValue())) { ❶
                switch (status.getState()) {
                    case TASK_RUNNING: ❷
                        j.started();
                        break;
                    case TASK_FINISHED: ❸
                        j.succeed();
                        break;
                    case TASK_FAILED: ❹
                    case TASK_KILLED: ❺
                    case TASK_LOST: ❻
                    case TASK_ERROR: ❼
                        j.fail();
                        break;
                    default:
                        break;
                }
            }
        }
    }
}
```

❶ Typically, one should store a mapping between the TaskID and the Job, rather than doing a linear search.

❷ This task status, *running*, means that we've received confirmation that the task was successfully started by the slave.

❸ A *finished* task is one that completed without reporting any kind of error.

❹ *Failed* tasks are those that did not complete successfully, and whose termination was initiated through a normal codepath by the task itself. For example, if a task that is supposed to download a file wasn't able to do so, it should report its status as failed.

❺ *Killed* tasks are those that did not complete successfully because the scheduler told them to stop. When a scheduler performs preemption or allows a user to request the early termination of a task, that task should report the status killed.

❻ When a task is *lost*, that means that an unexpected error occurred. That could be due to the slave unexpectedly going offline, or an executor that exited before it sent a TASK_FINISHED, TASK_KILLED, or TASK_KILLED message.

❼ This is a very rare case, indicating a problem with the task descriptor itself. You can look in the TaskStatus's message field for details.

Adding High Availability

At this point, our scheduler-only framework is nearly feature-complete. We are loading jobs from configuration files, launching them on Mesos, and automatically restarting them when they fail. Now it's time to add the final feature: high availability.

High availability means that when the scheduler process fails, the framework as a whole continues to run. This is accomplished via the cooperation of three subfeatures:

1. The scheduler will use leader election so that we can run multiple instances and have a fallback instance automatically take over when the current leader fails.
2. The scheduler must synchronize its state to shared, distributed storage, so that the newly elected leader can pick up where the last one left off.
3. The scheduler must opt into a few Mesos features that will ensure that running tasks are unaffected by scheduler failure.

For this example, we're going to use ZooKeeper to provide our leader election and distributed storage, since Mesos clusters usually[5] come with a ZooKeeper cluster. Furthermore, we're going to use the Apache Curator (*http://curator.apache.org*) library to interact with ZooKeeper, since it handles many of the challenges of the included ZooKeeper API.[6] Since this isn't meant to be a production-quality framework, we'll hardcode all our framework's data to reside under the /sampleframework path in ZooKeeper. For production-quality frameworks, you should make the location of all data configurable in ZooKeeper. Example 4-13 shows how we add basic leader election to our main function.

---

5 There's ongoing work to enable etcd as a ZooKeeper alternative. The issue is tracked on the Apache Mesos Jira as MESOS-1806 (*https://issues.apache.org/jira/browse/MESOS-1806*).

6 The examples in the book are written against Curator 2.7.1, using curator-framework and curator-recipes.

Example 4-13. Simple leader election

```
public static void main(String ... args) throws Exception {
    CuratorFramework curator = CuratorFrameworkFactory.newClient( ❶
            args[0],
            new RetryOneTime(1000)
    );
    curator.start(); ❷

    LeaderLatch leaderLatch = new LeaderLatch(curator, "/sampleframework/leader"); ❸
    leaderLatch.start(); ❹
    leaderLatch.await(); ❺

    // The previous main implementation goes here
}
```

❶ Here, we see how to create a new instance of Curator. It takes the address of the ZooKeeper cluster and a `RetryPolicy` as arguments. While we are using the `RetryOneTime` policy in this book, this is probably not the right choice for production frameworks. Instead, the `ExponentialBackoffRetry` or `BoundedExponentialBackoffRetry` policies are more robust choices.

❷ Note that you must explicitly `start()` the Curator framework.[7]

❸ Next, we create a `LeaderLatch` for our framework, which we'll put under the ZooKeeper path we chose for our framework, `/sampleframework`.

❹ Never forget to `start()` Curator components—this is the #1 pitfall.

❺ The `await()` method on a started `LeaderLatch` will not return until we are the leader.

---

7 Somewhat confusingly, the Apache Curator's API is also called a framework; however, it's completely unrelated to Mesos frameworks!

LeaderLatch Is Nice, but LeaderSelector Is Better

A `LeaderLatch` is a very easy way to add leader election to an application. You simply call `await()`, and when it returns, you're the leader! Unfortunately, if you do this, your application will not always behave correctly. Leaders can be deposed not only when they crash, but also when they are disconnected from the network. As a result, a properly implemented user of leader election needs to be constantly checking whether it's still the leader, and then recreating the leader latch after it's deposed. A better option for building robust leader election is `LeaderSelector`, another class in Curator. `LeaderSelector` has a listener-based API that notifies you whenever you become the leader or lose leadership. This book doesn't use `LeaderSelector` because it requires substantially more scaffolding code to use.

Unfortunately, it's not enough to simply allow multiple instances of our framework to elect a leader from amongst themselves. Our goal is to have the new leader actually become the same framework as before. To do this, we'll need to inform Mesos that our scheduler supports failover. In addition, when the new leader registers, it needs to tell Mesos that it's the new scheduler for our framework. In Mesos, schedulers are identified by their `FrameworkID`, an optional value in the `FrameworkInfo`. The `FrameworkID` must be assigned by Mesos in order to ensure it remains unique for each framework. Now, we'll need to actually store the `FrameworkID` when it's assigned, so that future leaders can reuse it.

We're going to store the `FrameworkID` in the ZooKeeper node `id` under our `/sampleframework` path. When we start up, we'll first check to see if there's already a saved `FrameworkID`; if so, we'll start up using that. Otherwise, we'll operate as before, and allow the Mesos master to assign a `FrameworkID` (see Example 4-14). In addition, we will store whatever `FrameworkID` Mesos informs us we registered with, so that future leaders can reuse that ID. We can store that `FrameworkID` unconditionally, since it will never change after the first assignment, and thus is idempotent.[8]

Example 4-14. Using a stored FrameworkID with FrameworkInfo

```
FrameworkInfo.Builder frameworkInfoBuilder = FrameworkInfo.newBuilder()
    .setUser("")
    .setName("Useless Remote BASH"); ❶
```

---

8 Operations that are idempotent have the same effect no matter whether you do them once or a thousand times. When building distributed systems, trying to make as many operations idempotent as possible reduces the chances of race conditions or unpredictable behavior when the network reorders and drops messages.

```
try {
    byte[] curatorData = curator.getData().forPath("/sampleframework/id"); ❷
    frameworkInfoBuilder.setId(new String(curatorData, "UTF-8"));
} catch (KeeperException.NoNodeException e) {
    // Don't set the FrameworkID ❸
}

FrameworkInfo frameworkInfo = frameworkInfoBuilder
    .setFailoverTimeout(60*60*24*7) ❹
    .build();
```

❶ We start with our builder, the same as usual.

❷ We attempt to fetch the stored FrameworkID. If this node doesn't exist in Zoo-
    Keeper, we throw a KeeperException.NoNodeException.

❸ If there wasn't a stored FrameworkID, we allow Mesos to assign it.

❹ We must configure the framework to have a failover timeout, in seconds. In this
    case, we allow failover to happen for up to a week. This means we've got a week
    to reconnect a new scheduler for this framework after shutting down the previ-
    ous scheduler. This timeout should be set to help you survive a worst-case sce-
    nario when you need enough time to recover the system after a catastrophe. After
    this timeout, requests to register with the old FrameworkID will be met with an
    error about registering a finished framework, and all tasks that were running
    under that framework will be killed.

Now, we need to update our registered scheduler callback to store the FrameworkID.
The new version is shown in Example 4-15.

Example 4-15. Storing the FrameworkID

```
public void registered(SchedulerDriver driver, FrameworkID frameworkId,
                            MasterInfo masterInfo) {
    System.out.println("Registered with framework id " + frameworkId);
    try {
        curator.create().creatingParentsIfNeeded().forPath( ❶
            "/sampleframework/id",
            frameworkId.getBytes()
        );
    } catch (KeeperException.NodeExistsException e) {
        // Do nothing ❷
    }
}
```

❶ We attempt to store the data of the FrameworkID to the predetermined location.

❷ If we catch this exception, it means that we've already created the node /sampleframework/id. In this case, we'll assume that means an earlier leader scheduler already stored the ID, so we'll do nothing. If you're using a different store than ZooKeeper, it may be more convenient to simply unconditionally store the ID every time, since it will never change.

Now, we've finally got a highly available framework with failover working. Or at least, we would if the framework had any way to also synchronize its state with regard to which jobs are running. To do this, we'll need to add support for serializing and deserializing jobs from ZooKeeper. We'll store each job in ZooKeeper at /sampleframework/jobs/$jobid, where $jobid is the id field of the job. Serialization can be trivially implemented via JSON.

Now that our framework is highly available, we don't want to always have to provide the set of jobs it should run. In fact, we'd like to have our framework automatically pick up the monitoring of all previously provided jobs on the command line, and also optionally launch new jobs provided on the command line. To do this, we'll load jobs both from the command line (if provided) and from ZooKeeper, as shown in Example 4-16.

Example 4-16. Loading job data

```
List<Job> jobs = new ArrayList<>(); ❶

if (args.length > 1) { ❷
    byte[] data = Files.readAllBytes(Paths.get(args[1]));
    JSONObject config = new JSONObject(new String(data, "UTF-8"));
    JSONArray jobsArray = config.getJSONArray("jobs");
    for (int i = 0; i < jobsArray.length(); i++) {
        jobs.add(Job.fromJSON(jobsArray.getJSONObject(i), curator));
    }
    System.out.println("Loaded jobs from file");
}

//Load jobs from ZK
try {
    for (String id : curator.getChildren().forPath("/sampleframework/jobs")) { ❸
        byte[] data = curator.getData()
                             .forPath("/sampleframework/jobs/" + id); ❹
        JSONObject jobJSON = new JSONObject(new String(data, "UTF-8"));
        Job job = Job.fromJSON(jobJSON, curator); ❺
        jobs.add(job);
    }
    System.out.println("Loaded jobs from ZK");
} catch (Exception e) {
    // Sample code isn't production ready ❻
}
```

❶ We start by creating the List we'll store all the Jobs in.

❷ We only run the original job loading code if a filename was passed on the command line.

❸ The getChildren() method in Curator allows us to get the names of all the child nodes of a path. These child nodes are saved after most state-changing methods, such as launch(), started(), and succeed().

❹ For each job, we'll fetch the serialized JSON representation from ZooKeeper.

❺ At this point, we can use the original JSON processing code to deserialize the Job. Note that we must provide every Job with a reference to the Curator now, since the Jobs must serialize themselves.

❻ In real production code, you should probably handle exceptions.

We'll also need to enhance our Jobs to be able to save their state, as shown in Example 4-17.

Example 4-17. Job serialization

```java
public class Job {
    // Previously defined fields elided
    private String id; ❶

    private void saveState() { ❷
        JSONObject obj = new JSONObject();
        obj.put("id", id); ❸
        obj.put("status", (status == JobState.STAGING ?
            JobState.RUNNING : status).toString()); ❹
        // Storing other fields omitted for brevity
        byte[] data = obj.toString().getBytes("UTF-8");
        try { ❺
            curator.setData().forPath("/sampleframework/jobs/" + id, data);
        } catch (KeeperException.NoNodeException e) {
            curator.create()
                    .creatingParentsIfNeeded()
                    .forPath("/sampleframework/jobs/" + id, data);
        }
    }
```

```
    public void launch() {
        // ... previous code omitted ...
        saveState(); ❻
    }

    // started(), succeed(), fail() are modified as above
}
```

❶ We need to include an identifier for each job, so that they can be looked up by a primary key in the database we sync them to.

❷ We've added a method to save the state of the Job to an external store. In this case, we're storing the JSON-formatted data to ZooKeeper.

❸ We need to make sure to store all the fields to the database.

❹ We always store jobs that are in STAGING as if they were running. Since we can't be sure whether a job in the STAGING state has launched successfully, we'll assume it succeeded during a failover, so that we'll either get a new statusUpdate if it finished in the meantime or a TASK_LOST after reconciliation.

❺ Curator's API requires a different method to create a new ZooKeeper node and update its data.

❻ We need to make sure to save the Job's state after every status update. Note that the addition of saveState() to the last line of started(), succeed(), and fail() is omitted in this code, but this must be done for a working framework.

And there you have it! Our job scheduler is now able to automatically fail over to waiting hot spares without impacting the running jobs or losing track of them—well, almost.

Adding Reconciliation

It turns out that there are still situations in which things can fall out of synchronization: these cases are explained in "Reconciliation During Failover" on page 127. This is the final piece missing from our robust, highly available Mesos scheduler. Luckily, it's easy to add reconciliation to a scheduler. When implementing the statusUpdate() callback, you are mapping the Mesos state events to your framework's state machine model. As long as this state machine never moves out of the terminal states (e.g., TASK_LOST, TASK_FINISHED, TASK_KILLED, etc.), reconciliation shouldn't require additional work. Typically, you'll want to run reconciliation periodically; I usually just run it on startup and every 30 minutes thereafter. Reconciliation is a sort of catchall for any message loss—it ensures that even if some unknown bug or hardware failure causes your framework to fall out of sync with the state of the Mesos cluster, you'll eventually correct that issue.

To reconcile, we will just generate a list of running tasks, along with the ID of the slave that they're running on (for an explanation of why, see "Reconciliation During Failover" on page 127). Then, we'll invoke reconcileTasks(). Mesos will automatically send the responses to the statusUpdate() callback. If you want to implement special handling of reconciliation-related status updates, you can check if the reason field of the status update is TASK_RECONCILIATION. We don't bother with that in our framework, because our framework's task state machine is robust. Example 4-18 shows how to reconcile the running tasks.

Example 4-18. Reconciliation of running tasks

```
List<TaskStatus> runningTasks = new ArrayList<>();
for (Job job : jobs) {
    if (job.getStatus() == JobState.RUNNING) {
        TaskID id = TaskID.newBuilder().setValue(job.getId()).build();
        SlaveID slaveId = SlaveID.newBuilder().setValue(job.getSlaveId()).build(); ❶
        System.out.println("Reconciling the task " + job.getId());
        runningTasks.add(TaskStatus.newBuilder()
                .setSlaveId(slaveId)
                .setTaskId(id)
                .setState(TaskState.TASK_RUNNING)
                .build());
    }
}
driver.reconcileTasks(runningTasks);
```

❶ Although we didn't show the code for it, we must record the ID of the slave we believe each task is currently running on so that we can perform reconciliation.

At last, we have a complete implementation of a highly available Mesos scheduler that is robust to all kinds of failures: masters can crash, slaves can be disconnected from the network, and the scheduler itself can be killed and restarted. In spite of any of those problems, the framework will endure, continually tracking, monitoring, and ensuring its tasks complete successfully. We accomplished this through several means:

Jobs over tasks

We separated the notion of a job that we'd like to run from the Mesos task. This allowed us to manage retries of a job, since the job's success or failure wasn't tied to a single attempt to run it. This conceptual framework works equally well for long-running services: a service is a *goal* to run some number of instances of a program; a task is an instance, but it could fail and be replaced with another task. If you're interested in learning more about using goals to handle the reliability of scalable, distributed systems, this idea was pioneered by Joe Armstrong in his thesis on building reliable telephone systems.[9]

Persistent framework identity

We enabled different schedulers to automatically fail over by storing the identity of our framework: the `FrameworkID`. This is the one part of framework management that we must do out-of-band from Mesos, since it must be propagated in spite of failures even within Mesos itself.

Shared job state

Whenever we received updates about the state of a job, we synchronized those updates with our distributed store of choice, ZooKeeper. This ensured that newly elected leader schedulers would have the best possible information about the state of the cluster.

Retries for jobs

Sometimes, a Mesos slave machine just doesn't work: perhaps it was misconfigured, or perhaps another task running on that slave is affecting its neighbors through a type of resource that Mesos can't isolate. To defend against these cases, we should always retry our actions. However, usually we also want to give up if a job keeps failing, since that may indicate a problem with the job itself.

Reconciliation

Ultimately, things will go wrong that we didn't predict. In an attempt to handle these events (or at least eventually recover from them automatically), we used the Mesos reconciliation API to periodically attempt to clarify our state. Although even reconciliation won't handle every such issue, it is the best tool we have for handling unknown unknowns.

Advanced Scheduler Techniques

Although we've managed to implement a feature-complete, reliable scheduler, there are many other ways in which we could add features and robustness to our scheduler. In this section, we'll discuss further improvements that production-quality schedulers should consider implementing.

---

9 Joe Armstrong, the author of Making reliable distributed systems in the presence of software errors (*http://www.erlang.org/download/armstrong_thesis_2003.pdf*), is also the creator of Erlang. Even though most of us aren't using Erlang, his ideas about goal-oriented programming and supervision pervade all reliable distributed systems, including Mesos and its close cousin from Google, Borg.

Distributed Communication

In our Useless Remote BASH, we only handled new jobs when a scheduler that had just become the leader was passed a file containing JSON job descriptors. In real schedulers, we'll want to be able to receive new jobs at any time. Most commonly, work will be communicated to our scheduler via an HTTP API.

If you decide to allow your scheduler to receive work over HTTP, it's better if both the leader and hot spare schedulers are all able to process HTTP requests. This can be accomplished in several ways:

Shared database
> In this design, the leader and hot spare schedulers all are able to read from and write to a shared database. This way, they can all serve client requests. Whenever a client modifies the database, however, we must ensure that the leading scheduler is notified. Some databases support notifications; if your database doesn't support this, the leading scheduler can frequently poll the database for updates so that it never lags too far behind the clients' instructions. The other solution for notifications is to use the leader election subsystem to identify the current leader, and then make a remote procedure call (RPC) to that leader so that it updates itself.

Redirect modification requests
> HTTP already supports redirection. In this case, leader and hot spare schedulers can handle read-only requests, but requests that update the state of the framework can simply be redirected to the leading master with a 302 Found response.

The data is the truth
> This pattern is similar to the shared database pattern, but rather than providing an HTTP API, clients communicate directly with the data layer, and the scheduler is totally subservient to whatever data is in the data layer. For instance, if you used Redis or RabbitMQ as your data layer, any client could add work to it, and the leading scheduler would periodically poll for new tasks it needs to launch and replicate all status updates to the data layer.

In practice, most framework authors reach for ZooKeeper first. ZooKeeper is a great choice for many types of frameworks, for the following reasons:

- It provides leader election primitives.
- It stores arbitrary data.
- It supports arbitrary transactions.
- It's highly available.
- It can notify clients when data changes.

- A Mesos cluster already has an instance.

ZooKeeper's main downside is that it can't scale to hundreds of thousands of data elements. For that use case, you'll need to sacrifice the strong consistency it provides for other data stores like Cassandra, Redis, or MySQL.

Forced Failover

At some point, you may want to make a framework that automatically forces failover to a new scheduler. This could be useful in two cases:

1. Your scheduler knows what the current running version is and will trigger a failover if it is a newer version, to simplify the upgrade process.

2. Your scheduler starts out running on the user's command line, but it actually creates a task on the Mesos cluster that will take over for the command-line tool. For example, mesos-submit (*http://bit.ly/mesos-submit*) (now deprecated) did this.

If you want to trigger a failover, simply register your new scheduler with the existing FrameworkID. When Mesos accepts the new scheduler's registration, it will trigger the error() callback of the old scheduler, with the message Framework failover. Unfortunately, this message string is the only way to distinguish a purposeful failover from an actual framework error.

Consolidating Offers

One issue that some schedulers run into is offer fragmentation. Offer fragmentation occurs when multiple frameworks are connected to the Mesos cluster, and one of them launches multiple tasks of similar (but not the same) size. Usually, the Mesos master can consolidate free resources from each host. Fragmentation occurs when the master isn't able to do so. The root cause is that the various fractions of the resources are repeatedly being offered to different connected frameworks, and thus are never idle long enough to consolidate. This can manifest as, for example, a host having eight offers with one CPU each, rather than one eight-CPU offer. To solve this problem, your framework must change the way it handles offers: rather than immediately using or declining offers, it can hold on to them temporarily in order to wait and see if any more offers come in on those hosts. Remember, when you call launchTasks, you can pass it as many offers for the same slave as you'd like (see the note Combining Offers following Example 4-5).

You can build offer consolidation as a form of middleware for your resourceOffers callback. Instead of calling your original implementation of resourceOffers, first put all new offers into a map, keyed by slave, so that you can track all the offers for each slave. Then, you can decide when to remove a group of offers from the map and pass them to your original resourceOffers callback. When doing this, you should also make sure that you can't accidentally hold on to an offer forever—you should still try to decline offers after a couple of minutes, to keep the whole cluster operating smoothly.

There are two broad classes of strategies for deciding when you should pass a group of offers along to the original `resourceOffers` implementation: you can pass along a group when it's *big enough*, or when it's been *long enough*. If you choose the *big enough* strategy, you'll need to keep track of the biggest task that you need to launch. Then, when you finally receive enough offers on a single slave to satisfy the task, you can pass along the group of offers to the code that will launch the task. If you choose the *long enough* strategy, you'll also need to choose how long to hold on to an offer (typically, 15–60 seconds). Then, when an offer is held for longer than the chosen time, you can pass all of that slave's offers to your original `resourceOffers`, and hopefully that group will be big enough.

The benefit of the big enough strategy is that you're guaranteed to launch your task when you find enough offers. The downsides are that you still need to worry about liveness (occasionally declining old offers), and you need to track the size of pending tasks. The strategy becomes even more complicated if you'd like to try to pack multiple tasks into an offer group, as you now need to keep track of many variables: the offers on each slave, the pending tasks, and the different ways those tasks could be packed into the offers.

On the other hand, the long enough strategy is simpler to implement: you don't need to worry about the task sizes at all; instead, you are assuming that you will eventually receive enough offers during the time window you chose to satisfy any pending task. The downside of this strategy is that it could struggle to launch a very big task, since if you waited longer, you could've received the last necessary offer to succeed.

Ultimately, consolidating offers is not necessary until you reach a certain scale on your Mesos cluster. It is, however, good to know how to diagnose this problem, and how to design a solution to it. In production Mesos clusters I've operated, we've run into this problem and solved it successfully using the long enough strategy.

Fenzo, a Scheduling Library

Fenzo (*https://github.com/Netflix/Fenzo*) is a library released by Netflix in the summer of 2015. For Java-based schedulers, Fenzo provides a complete solution to offer buffering, multiple task launching, and hard and soft constraint matching. Many, if not most, schedulers would probably benefit from using Fenzo to compute task assignments, rather than writing the offer buffering, packing, and placement routines themselves.

Hardening Your Scheduler

In our example scheduler, we simply retry jobs on the next offer that we receive once they've failed. Often, some job won't run on a particular host due to some uniquely broken aspect of that host. To protect against this type of repeated failure, you should track which hosts a job has failed on, and not retry the job on those hosts. In practice, this protects against all kinds of host misconfiguration.

A job not working on a particular host isn't the only host-related issue you could encounter. Rarely (but what's rare at scale?), you'll get a *black hole host*: a host that causes every job it runs to fail, often extremely quickly. Black hole hosts will rapidly exhaust all the retries for all the jobs you're trying to run, resulting in spurious failures that require manual intervention. To handle black hole hosts, you should track how many failures you've seen on each host in the past minute. If that number exceeds some predetermined target, then you should stop accepting offers from that host entirely. Some frameworks expect tasks to never fail (like long-running services), so seeing 20 failures from a single host in a minute bodes poorly for it. On the other hand, some frameworks complete thousands of tasks every second; for these, 20 failures on a single host in a minute would be totally normal, and so they'd only blacklist a host after thousands of failures in a short duration. Finally, when implementing a blacklist, make sure that you can receive notifications when hosts are blacklisted, and make sure that those hosts are automatically unblacklisted after a week. If you don't automatically notify and later unblock these hosts, you could accidentally forget about them and leave those resources idling forever, costing money but not doing any work. Alternatively, you can use an automated system like Satellite (*https://github.com/twosigma/satellite*) to handle this situation for all frameworks.

Framework UI

Usually, frameworks have a web UI, since the browser is such a powerful platform for graphical interfaces. The `FrameworkInfo` protobuf has a field called `webui_url` that should be set to the URL that the UI is available on. When you set this field, the Mesos UI will make the framework's name in the UI a link to the provided `webui_url`. If you use this feature, you should either ensure that the `webui_url` is managed behind a load balancer, or update it in the `FrameworkInfo` every time a new scheduler becomes the leader.

Allocating Ports

We only used scalar resources in our scheduler (i.e., CPUs and memory). Mesos also supports range-type resources, the most common of which is ports. Mesos manages the ports on the cluster to ensure that each task that needs to listen on a socket binds to a unique port, and to ensure that tasks that require specific ports won't start on slaves for which those ports are already in use. The available ports are encoded as a list of [*begin, end*] pairs of available ports; to use them, you simply add the sub-ranges you're interested in as resources. For example, in Example 4-19 we demonstrate a function, findNPorts, that finds *N* ports from the given offer and returns the resources that should be added to the TaskInfo that needs those ports.

Example 4-19. Port allocation

```
public static Resource findNPorts(Offer offer, int n) {
    int numStillNeeded = n;
    Value.Ranges.Builder ranges = Value.Ranges.newBuilder();
    List<Value.Range> availablePorts = null;

    for (Resource r : offer.getResourcesList()) {
        if (r.getName().equals("ports")) {
            availablePorts = r.getRanges().getRangeList();  ❶
        }
    }

    while (numStillNeeded > 0 &&
                availablePorts != null &&
                !availablePorts.isEmpty()) {  ❷
        Value.Range portRange = availablePorts.remove(0);  ❸
        long numAvail = portRange.getEnd() - portRange.getBegin() + 1;  ❹
        long numWillUse = numAvail >= numStillNeeded ?
                numStillNeeded : numAvail;  ❺
        ranges.addRange(Value.Range.newBuilder()
                .setBegin(portRange.getBegin())
                .setEnd(portRange.getBegin() + numWillUse - 1)  ❻
                .build());
        numStillNeeded -= numWillUse;
    }

    if (numStillNeeded > 0) {  ❼
        throw new RuntimeException("Couldn't satisfy " + n + " ports");
    }

    return Resource.newBuilder()
        .setName("ports")
        .setType(Value.Type.RANGES)
        .setRanges(ranges.build())
        .build();
}
```

❶ We first find the Ranges that contain the available ports.

❷ We will keep looking for ports as long as there are still available ports and we need them.

❸ We will check the contiguous subranges one at a time.

❹ The contiguous subranges are inclusive; thus, if the subrange is [10-20], there are actually 11 ports available.

❺ When deciding how many ports to use from this subrange, we will never exceed how many we still need or how many are available.

❻ Remember that the range is inclusive, and beware the off-by-one error!

❼ It's possible that we couldn't find enough ports; better to blow up than return bad data.

Besides ranges, which can be tricky to work with, Mesos also has set-type resources. Sets of resources currently only exist when defined on the slave command line. They are represented as lists in the Resource protobuf, and they're straightforward to use. You can learn more about creating custom resource types in "Configuring Custom Resources" on page 16.

Checkpointing

Even though we should always strive to implement our frameworks to be robust against all kinds of errors, it's actually possible to instruct Mesos to checkpoint status updates from tasks onto disk, in case the update coincides with a slave restart. You can enable this by setting the checkpoint property of the FrameworkInfo to true. This turns some slave crashes and restarts into unexceptional behavior. I recommend always doing this, unless you expect to generate large numbers of status updates over short intervals. Since checkpointing causes every status update to be written to disk, if you make thousands of status updates per second per slave, that would incur thousands of additional disk I/O operations per second per slave, which could degrade cluster performance. You should benchmark your framework with and without checkpointing if you're concerned about its performance impact; otherwise, it's best to always use it.

CommandInfo

The CommandInfo protobuf describes how a process should be launched. We'll examine CommandInfo's two sides: fields related to launching a process, and fields related to setting up the environment for the process.

Launching a process

CommandInfo supports two ways to launch a process: through the execv syscall, and via the system's default shell (such as Dash or Bash). If you want to launch your process using execv, this will ensure that you can control the arguments to your process very precisely, and not worry about how shells interpret strings. To launch the process directly, set the `value` to be the path to the executable, set the `arguments` to be the args array, and set `shell` to `false`. If you'd like it to be launched via a shell, however (so that you can use shell operators like `&&`, `||`, and `|` to compose programs), you must set `shell` to `true`, and then the entire contents of the `value` will be invoked by running `/bin/sh -c "$value"`; `arguments` are ignored for shell commands.

Configuring the process's environment

Mesos allows you to control three additional aspects of the process's environment: the user account that it runs as (via the `user` field, subject to the ACLs), the environment variables that the process sees (via the `environment` field, which is just a list of name/value pairs wrapped into a protobuf), and the filesystem state (via URIs). This last parameter requires additional explanation: it allows you to specify any number of URIs that should be downloaded into the executor sandbox (the current working directory when the executor starts running). You can choose whether those URIs should be executable, which is useful because you can instruct your `CommandInfo` to bootstrap and install the application's binaries directly into the sandbox, obviating the need for a deployment system. You can also specify whether to extract archive files, as Mesos understands those extensions and can download and unpack the application or additional resources automatically. The extensions recognized are currently *.tgz*, *.tar.gz*, *.tbz2*, *.tar.bz2*, *.txz*, *.tar.xz*, and *.zip*. By default, Mesos supports the URI schemes *hdfs://*, *http://*, *https://*, *ftp://*, *ftps://*, and *file://* (for use with NFS or other networked POSIX filesystems), as well as any other URI schemes that the installed Hadoop client supports (Hadoop is not a required dependency, though, and *hdfs://* will simply fail if it's not installed). You can add support for additional means of fetching binary dependencies by modifying *src/launcher/fetcher.cpp* accordingly.

> The task's sandbox is always available in the environment variable `$MESOS_DIRECTORY`.

Summary

In this chapter, we learned how to implement the scheduler component of a Mesos framework. The scheduler is responsible for launching tasks, monitoring those tasks, and interacting with the user. Many frameworks only need to implement a scheduler; all the functionality necessary to build most distributed, scalable, clustered applications can be implemented by orchestrating the launching of worker processes. We looked at a few example framework architectures, such as the pool of servers scheduler, work queue scheduler, and job processor scheduler. Then, we walked through the implementation of a job processor.

To build the job processor scheduler, we had to use a database, ZooKeeper, to persist the state of the application. Even though the scheduler API has many callbacks, we only needed to implement a handful of them to create a working system. We separated the notion of jobs (what the user wants to do) from tasks (code that Mesos runs on the cluster). This separation allowed us to easily build retries into our scheduler. The scheduler also needed a basic optimization, offer packing, in order to avoid being too slow.

Once the scheduler was up and running, we added high availability by combining an external leader election library, Curator, with additional features of the Mesos framework registration API. Unfortunately, once we gained the ability to fail over, we opened ourselves up to the possible loss of task status updates. To resolve this, we implemented task reconciliation, which allowed the scheduler to always behave correctly during planned and unplanned failover scenarios.

After learning how to implement a reliable Mesos scheduler, we discussed additional considerations for production-quality frameworks should. Since we usually have many instances of a scheduler running, and only one is the master, we looked at several designs for how clients can interact with the schedulers. We learned about offer fragmentation, what causes it, and some strategies to ensure that a framework never fails to find big enough offers. Besides CPUs and memory, many frameworks must allocate ports to their tasks: we learned about range-type resources, and how port allocation differs from CPU and memory scalar allocation. Finally, we briefly discussed issues such as building a user interface for a framework, hardening a framework against unknowns, and automating failovers during maintenance.

At this point, you're fully equipped to write a Mesos framework that can launch and monitor tasks, handle various types of failures and unexpected scenarios, and operate efficiently on your cluster. Next, we'll learn about how to increase the capabilities of frameworks by implementing custom executors, which will allow things like dynamically resizing containers and allowing tasks to share resources.

CHAPTER 5

Building a Mesos Executor

Now you've seen how to build a scheduler for Mesos. However, there are some things that can't be done with the scheduler API alone. For instance, perhaps you'd like to run several tasks in the same container. Maybe your application has lifecycle messages for the scheduler, reporting on its progress or application-specific statistics. Or perhaps you'd like to layer additional functionality into the executed task. In order to accomplish these things, you need to write a custom Mesos executor.

This is what we'll learn how to do in this chapter. Initially, we'll simply provide the functionality of the built-in CommandExecutor, which we learned about at the end of the last chapter. Then, we'll add support for heartbeats to enable faster failure detection. Finally, we'll discuss potential designs for progress reporting, improved logging, and running multiple tasks in the same container.

The Executor

We've already learned what a scheduler is: it's the component that interacts with the Mesos masters and the framework's clients, manages the running tasks, and handles failovers. But what is an executor? An executor has three responsibilities:

- Executing tasks as requested by the scheduler
- Keeping the scheduler informed of the status of those tasks
- Handling other requests from the scheduler

You Probably Don't Want to Do This

Writing executors is very tedious. Unfortunately, the only way to test whether the communication between your scheduler and executors is working is to start a new instance of your framework on a Mesos cluster. Furthermore, correctly implementing health checks, process management, and concurrency is very tricky. I strongly encourage you to think about how you could leverage the `CommandExecutor` rather than building your own executor. Nevertheless, there are many problems that can only be solved by writing an executor.

Building a Work Queue's Worker

Recall that the work queue scheduler needs individual workers to execute the work items. When we discussed it earlier, I suggested using an external queuing system, like Redis or RabbitMQ, that your worker processes could connect with directly, but that's not the only way to build it. Using a custom executor, you could instead send tasks directly to the executor. If you're using RabbitMQ or Redis, there's not much advantage to doing this; however, if you chose to store your state in a database like Postgres, you might not be able to easily scale to thousands of connections from every worker. As a result, you could instead simply have the scheduler send multiple tasks to the same executor.

This has upsides and downsides. On the one hand, it could allow you to avoid adding yet another piece of infrastructure (a queuing layer) to solve your scaling problems. On the other hand, it's now your responsibility to implement the queuing semantics you want in your scheduler, which is much more challenging than relying on battle-tested queues.

Running Pickled Tasks

What Is a Pickled Task?

Serialized code or configuration data that represents a task is known as a pickled task. For example, sending RPCs requires a way to serialize a task's parameters so that it can be transmitted across the network. Many languages support sending bytecode, executable source code, or other data. The term "pickle" comes from Python's serialization library.

Many of us are using the Java Virtual Machine (JVM) or Docker to run our code. Due to their potentially long initialize time, we may want to provide generated code to an executor. For example, it might take 45 seconds to start a JVM with all the classes we need: this is not something we'd like to do thousands of times per second. In order to avoid the 45-second overhead for each task, it'd be nice to reuse the JVMs for tasks on the same host. With a custom executor, it is possible to read raw bytes from each task and deserialize them into executable code. Then, the executor can simply run that code, reusing the whole JVM. For short tasks, this could be the difference between a task taking 10 seconds or 55 seconds: this is one of the tricks that enables Spark's low latency.

This approach can also be used to partially mitigate the challenge of writing an executor: you need only write the "pickle executor" once. After you've written it, you can benefit from the dynamic resizability of the executor (see "Multiple Tasks" on page 119), and you won't need to debug the communications again. Note that this doesn't require building a custom executor—you could also communicate pickled tasks through an out-of-band mechanism; the only downside is that you'd lose the ability to dynamically resize the container.

Sharing Resources

Imagine writing an application where each task reads a large static dataset and a small user-provided dataset, crunches the numbers, and returns the result. This could be used for running a series of simulations or training a machine learning model. A custom executor could be used to easily share a large static dataset, and still benefit from Mesos's resource accounting and automatic cleanup when the executor terminates. To do this, you could configure the custom executor to initialize itself by downloading the large dataset into its sandbox and reserving enough memory for it to remain in the Filesystem's in-memory block cache. Then, the tasks you launch on that executor could memory map that dataset, so that they get in-memory, direct access. This approach would reduce the bandwidth and disk costs of copying that dataset more times than necessary.

Another time that a custom executor could share resources is when building general purpose graphics processing unit (GPGPU) applications. Frequently, you'll only have one GPGPU in each slave. If you used the CommandExecutor and made the GPGPU a custom resource (see "Configuring Custom Resources" on page 16), you'd only be able to run one task at a time on each slave; however, you might want to manage the sharing of that GPGPU in an application-specific way. To do that, you could use the pickled tasks pattern described in the previous section to ensure each task programmatically exposes when it needs to use the GPGPU. Then, the custom executor could run all the tasks within the same container, so that it can broker and scheduler the tasks' use of the GPGPU.

These are just a few examples of the ways in which you might want to try to share resources between tasks. Of course, there are many other ways in which tasks can share their work, from common subproblems to shared caches. Sometimes, the most efficient way to take advantage of these structures is to run them in the same container, which requires writing an executor.

Better Babysitting

Mesos is engineered to maximize availability: when a scheduler crashes, it can automatically fail over; when a slave is upgraded, executors can automatically reconnect to the new version; when a network link goes down, the slave and executors continue to run with their last known instructions. For some applications, however, this isn't actually the behavior you want.

At large scale, partial and unexpected failures can reveal subtle bugs that weren't identified during testing and QA. To reduce the impact of these unknown, unpredictable issues, you can require that every executor checks in with the scheduler periodically, and if some executor misses too many check-ins, it can be presumed LOST by the scheduler.

Suppose that a slave loses connectivity to the scheduler, but not to its databases. An executor running on that slave might be able to continue uninterrupted, even though the scheduler can't receive messages when its tasks finish. This can cause the system to appear stuck to an administrator.

To solve this, we could add a heartbeating mechanism to the executor: the executor will periodically let the scheduler know it's still running, so that if an executor misses several heartbeats, the scheduler can presume the executor LOST and restart it on a healthy slave. This is known as babysitting—constant, active supervision that helps to detect failures faster. A custom executor can implement heartbeating functionality with the Mesos messaging APIs, ensuring that the overall system remains healthy.

Mesos-Native Heartbeating

In an upcoming version after 0.25, Mesos will add native support for three types of health checks—HTTP requests, TCP connection checks, and running a command. When these are enabled in the TaskInfo, they'll send periodic StatusUpdates. You might recognize these as the health checks that Marathon provides (see "Health Checks" on page 43). The Mesos project often integrates useful functionality from frameworks back into the core. See MESOS-2533 (*http://bit.ly/MESOS2533*) and MESOS-3567 (*http://bit.ly/MESOS3567*) for updates.

Augmented Logging

The final example of a custom executor's usefulness is in augmenting the logging facilities of Mesos. Mesos writes each process's stdout and stderr to local files in the executor sandbox. With a custom executor, the process's stdout and stderr can be forwarded to a centralized log repository or data storage location (such as HDFS, S3, or Logstash), allowing you to upgrade all CommandExecutor-based tasks to centrally store their logs. However, this could also be accomplished by running a log redirector such as logger (*http://linux.die.net/man/1/logger*), which connects a process's stdout to syslog, thus avoiding the need to make a custom executor.

Rewriting the CommandExecutor

Now that we've seen some examples of when we'd want to write an executor, let's take a look at how to actually do so. We're going to start by writing something very simple: an executor that is compatible with the built-in CommandExecutor.

We'll start by looking at the skeleton of MyExecutor, our CommandExecutor clone. The imports and class declaration are presented in Example 5-1.

Example 5-1. Imports and class declaration of MyExecutor

```
package com.example;
import org.apache.mesos.*;
import org.apache.mesos.Protos.*;
import java.util.*;
import java.io.File;
import org.json.*; ❶
import java.lang.ProcessBuilder.Redirect; ❷

public class MyExecutor implements Executor, Runnable { ❸
    // We'll discuss the inner bits as we go
}
```

❶ We'll use JSON to encode the task we want to run. This JSON will be read from the TaskInfo so that we know what to invoke.

❷ The ProcessBuilder is the most convenient way to start a process in Java; we'll use it to launch our application, and we'll redirect the application's stdout and stderr to separate log files from our executor.

❸ Since there's no callback API for finding out when a process finishes, we'll start a thread to wait for the process—that's why we implement Runnable.

The main method is shown in Example 5-2.

Example 5-2. main of MyExecutor

```
public static void main(String ... args) throws Exception {
    Executor executor = new MyExecutor();
    ExecutorDriver driver = new MesosExecutorDriver(executor);
    driver.run();
}
```

Although it's tempting to try to configure some things via the command line passed in to `main`, you'll be thankful that all executor configuration comes from the Mesos APIs—this will simplify development in the long run by ensuring all configuration comes from a single source. When the scheduler has total control over the executors, this simplifies development: global (scheduler) changes and local (executor) changes are now managed from a single codebase, the scheduler's. This makes developing new features easier, and it simplifies operations, since the administrators need only to modify and reload the scheduler to make framework-wide changes.

As with the scheduler, in the `main` of our executor we create a corresponding driver to communicate with Mesos. Unfortunately, this driver turns out to be a major annoyance. When the framework calls `MesosExecutorDriver.start()`, it needs to have been started by a slave. The slave injects an environment variable, `MESOS_SLAVE_PID`, which is used to allow the executor to connect to the slave that started it and begin participating in the Mesos protocols. As a result, if you want to test your executor, you need to implement a mock `ExecutorDriver`. If you forget to do this, you'll see a weird stack trace like this, regardless of what language you're developing your executor in:

```
F0605 21:32:01.538770 18480 os.hpp:173] Expecting 'MESOS_SLAVE_PID' in
environment variables
*** Check failure stack trace: ***
    @     0x7fc535912dfd  google::LogMessage::Fail()
    @     0x7fc535914c3d  google::LogMessage::SendToLog()
    @     0x7fc5359129ec  google::LogMessage::Flush()
    @     0x7fc535915539  google::LogMessageFatal::~LogMessageFatal()
    @     0x7fc5352c9ff0  os::getenv()
    @     0x7fc53534139b  mesos::MesosExecutorDriver::start()
    @     0x7fc5359068ee  Java_org_apache_mesos_MesosExecutorDriver_start
    @     0x7fc5390127f8  (unknown)
```

We'll block the main thread until our driver completes—when the task is finished, we'll call `driver.stop()` elsewhere to ensure the executor exits correctly. Since executors decouple the notion of tasks from the containers and processes that run them, it's easy to forget that sending a `TASK_FINISHED` doesn't terminate the executor. You should always have executors shut themselves down once they've finished their work, or have the scheduler explicitly manage their lifetime by killing their canary tasks (see "Canary tasks" on page 120).

Just like for schedulers, many of the executor callbacks aren't important to handle. Example 5-3 lists the callbacks we can ignore for now.

Example 5-3. Ignoring callbacks

```
public void frameworkMessage(ExecutorDriver driver, byte[] data) { } ❶
public void registered(ExecutorDriver driver, ExecutorInfo executorInfo, ❷
                       FrameworkInfo frameworkInfo, SlaveInfo slaveInfo) {
    System.out.println("registered executor " + executorInfo);
}
public void disconnected(ExecutorDriver driver) { } ❸
public void shutdown(ExecutorDriver driver) { } ❹
public void reregistered(ExecutorDriver driver, SlaveInfo slaveInfo) { } ❺
public void error(ExecutorDriver driver, java.lang.String message) { } ❻
```

❶ Framework messages are a simple (but not guaranteed, as we'll see in the upcoming sidebar) way to communicate between the scheduler and its executors by sending arbitrary data serialized as bytes. Note that framework messages aren't routed to particular tasks.

❷ This is invoked the first time that an executor connects to the slave. The most common thing to do is get data from the ExecutorInfo, since that can carry executor configuration information in its data field, which contains arbitrary bytes.

❸ This is invoked when the slave disconnects from the executor, which typically indicates a slave restart. Rarely should an executor need to do anything special here.

❹ This callback informs the executor to gracefully shut down. It is called when a slave restart fails to complete within the grace period, or when the executor's framework completes. The executor will be forcibly killed if shutdown doesn't complete within 5 seconds (the default, configurable on the slave command line with --executor_shutdown_grace_period).

❺ This callback is invoked after a successful slave restart; it contains the new slave's information.

❻ This callback is invoked after a fatal error occurs. When this callback is invoked, the driver is no longer running.

As you can see, the executor can actually be a full participant in the slave checkpointing and recovery system; however, you can ignore this for almost all executors. We'll make use of some of these callbacks later, but for now, let's continue by looking at how to actually launch a task.

Framework Messages Are Unreliable

sendFrameworkMessage is just a thin wrapper around the libprocess semantics (see "Libprocess and the Actor Model" on page 123 for details), so delivery isn't guaranteed. This means that if you use sendFrameworkMessage, your framework must not rely on any guaranteed delivery of messages—you need to handle retries yourself. But what's an unreliable delivery useful for, anyway? In spite of the lack of guarantees, the messages actually will be delivered in all but the most extreme failure conditions of the cluster. This means that sendFrameworkMessage is great for all sorts of advisory messages.

One such advisory message is a task heartbeat. Your scheduler wants to know whether its tasks are continuing to make progress, or whether they've stalled or become deadlocked for whatever reason. To detect this, simply send a framework message once per minute to the scheduler, and have the scheduler track which executors it hasn't heard from for 5 or 10 minutes. If a message is not delivered for some transient reason, we can assume the next one will probably succeed; however, if no messages are delivered over an extended period, that implies that there is a real issue with the executor (or that the network's having other problems). We'll learn how to implement this in "Adding Heartbeats" on page 113.

Another use for framework messages is for providing progress updates that will be consumed by users in the UI. There are many communication strategies that ensure that it's not problematic if one update is missed. For instance, if each update is a completion percentage, the latest update will always subsume earlier updates (since it should always be greater than or equal to the previous value). Generally, framework messages are good for progress reporting when newer updates supersede earlier ones, and the updates are being used for human, rather than programmatic, consumption.

We'll start by looking at what data we'll need to access throughout the executor's implementation. These are global variables that are defined in the MyExecutor class (see Example 5-1):

Process proc
> We'll need to store a reference to the process we launched so that we can wait for it to complete.

TaskID taskId
> We also need to communicate the task's status to Mesos: the driver API to communicate with our scheduler requires the TaskID as an argument.

```
ExecutorDriver driver
```
Of course, we'll want to be able to use the driver, so we'll store a reference to it as well.

Well-behaved executors should keep Mesos up-to-date with the status of their tasks. Since sending status updates has some boilerplate, we'll write a convenience method, shown in Example 5-4.

Example 5-4. Status update helper

```
private void statusUpdate(TaskState state) {
    TaskStatus status = TaskStatus.newBuilder()
        .setTaskId(taskId)
        .setState(state)
        .build()
    driver.sendStatusUpdate(status);
}
```

Here, we simply construct a bare-bones task status and send it via the driver. Sometimes, you'll want to communicate additional information. Like most Mesos protobufs, TaskStatus supports arbitrary data, as well as a human-readable message.

In order to keep this example simple, our executor will only support running a single task, after which it will exit. We'll enforce this invariant with a helper function, as seen in Example 5-5.

Example 5-5. Ensuring a single task

```
private boolean ensureOneLaunch(ExecutorDriver driver, TaskID id) { ❶
    if (this.taskId != null) { ❷
        TaskStatus status = TaskStatus.newBuilder()
            .setTaskId(id) ❸
            .setState(TaskState.TASK_ERROR)
            .setMessage("this executor only can run a single task") ❹
            .build();
        driver.sendStatusUpdate(status);
        return false;
    } else {
        return true;
    }
}
```

❶ We'll return true if this is the first task, and false if it should be ignored.

❷ The code that launches our task will set the value of this.taskId. Thus, we can assume that if this.taskId was already set, we've already launched a task, so this one is invalid.

❸ Note that we use the `TaskID` of the newly requested task, not the running task.

❹ We'll take advantage of the human-readable message in the status update to help the user diagnose why the task launch resulted in an error.

Example 5-6 illustrates how we actually launch a process. We'll take the configuration JSON object as an input, and we'll return the newly started process. To help separate our logs, we'll redirect the task process's `stdout` and `stderr` to different files than the executor's `stdout` and `stderr`. For now, the task JSON will have only a single key: `"cmd"`, which is the command line to run the task. We'll invoke the task with a shell for simplicity.

Example 5-6. Starting a process

```
private Process startProcess(JSONObject cfg) throws Exception{
    List<String> cmdArgs = Arrays.asList("bash", "-c", cfg.getString("cmd")); ❶
    ProcessBuilder pb = new ProcessBuilder(cmdArgs); ❷
    File stdoutFile = new File(System.getenv("MESOS_DIRECTORY"), "child_stdout"); ❸
    File stderrFile = new File(System.getenv("MESOS_DIRECTORY"), "child_stderr"); ❸
    pb.redirectOutput(Redirect.to(stdoutFile)); ❹
    pb.redirectError(Redirect.to(stderrFile)); ❹
    return pb.start();
}
```

❶ We build the argument vector for the process we will launch.

❷ The `ProcessBuilder` API is a simple way to launch a process in Java.

❸ The path to the executor's scratch space is placed into the environment variable `MESOS_DIRECTORY` by the slave. It's best to write any output into this directory, since it's automatically garbage collected when the slave needs to reclaim disk space after the executor exits.

❹ We redirect the task process's output.

At this point, we're finally ready to handle launching a task. To do so, we must implement the `launchTask` callback of the `Executor` interface (see Example 5-7).

Example 5-7. Implementing launchTask

```
public void launchTask(ExecutorDriver driver, TaskInfo task) {
    synchronized (this) { ❶
        try {
            if (!ensureOneLaunch(driver, task.getTaskId())) { ❷
                return;
            }
```

```
            this.taskId = task.getTaskId(); ❸
            this.driver = driver; ❸

            statusUpdate(TaskState.TASK_STARTING); ❹

            byte[] taskData = task.getData().toByteArray(); ❺
            JSONObject cfg = new JSONObject(new String(taskData, "UTF-8"));
            this.proc = startProcess(cfg); ❸ ❻

            statusUpdate(TaskState.TASK_RUNNING); ❹

            Thread t = new Thread(this); ❼
            t.setDaemon(true);
            t.start();
        } catch (Exception e) {
            e.printStackTrace(); ❽
        }
    }
}
```

❶ To protect access to all global variables, we put a mutex around all the concurrent code in the executor.[1]

❷ We check that this is the first task we've received. If it isn't, we'll do nothing and just return.

❸ We store a few things to which we have access in this callback into global variables: the TaskID, the ExecutorDriver, and the Process, as explained earlier.

❹ As we process the task, we keep Mesos informed of our progress.

❺ The details of the task must be extracted and parsed.

❻ Finally, we can start the process.

❼ We'll need to watch the process to know when it completes, and whether it completes successfully. We'll look at the implementation of this completion monitoring thread next.

❽ In real production code, you should try to make it easier to diagnose what goes wrong in executor code. This is easiest to do by also transmitting exceptions via StatusUpdate if they're fatal.

---

1 Java concurrency is beyond the scope of this book, so you'll just have to trust me that this works.

At this point, we nearly know the entirety of how our executor goes about managing the lifecycle of its task. Example 5-8 illustrates how we track the completion of the task.

Example 5-8. Waiting for the process to finish

```
public void run() {
    int exitCode;
    try {
        exitCode = proc.waitFor(); ❶
    } catch (Exception e) {
        exitCode = -99; ❷
    }
    synchronized (this) { ❸
        if (proc == null) { ❹
            return;
        }
        proc = null; ❺
        if (exitCode == 0) { ❻
            statusUpdate(TaskState.TASK_FINISHED);
        } else { ❼
            driver.sendStatusUpdate(TaskStatus.newBuilder()
                    .setTaskId(taskId)
                    .setState(TaskState.TASK_FAILED)
                    .setMessage("Process exited with code " + exitCode)
                    .build());
        }
    }
    driver.stop(); ❽
}
```

❶ waitFor() will block until the process terminates, and it returns the process's exit code.

❷ If waitFor() throws an exception for some reason, we'll assume something went terribly wrong and use a distinctive exit code to signal that.

❸ As mentioned before, the mutex on this protects access to the global variables.

❹ If we reach this point and proc is null, this is a special signal that means that process was killed by killTask (which we haven't seen yet). In that case, our work's already done.

❺ By setting proc to null, we set that special signal from above.

❻ When the process exits with a successful status, we report that the task finished (remember, FINISHED is a successful status in Mesos).

❼ Otherwise, we know that the task failed, and so we send a `FAILED` status.

❽ We `stop()` the executor driver at this point, so that our `main` function can return and the executor will gracefully shut down.

We've seen how our new executor handles accepting a task, starting a process, and sending the appropriate status updates when that process finishes. All we have left is to handle requests from the scheduler to kill the task early. Example 5-9 shows how to handle a `killTask` message.

Example 5-9. Implementation of killTask

```
public void killTask(ExecutorDriver driver, TaskID taskId) {
    synchronized (this) {  ❶
        if (proc != null  ❷
                && taskId.equals(this.taskId)) {  ❸
            proc.destroy();  ❹
            statusUpdate(TaskState.TASK_KILLED);  ❺
            proc = null;
        }
        driver.stop();
    }
}
```

❶ As mentioned before, we must protect all access to global variables with a mutex.

❷ If `proc` is `null`, then the process has already died, either because it finished or because of an earlier `killTask`.

❸ We should also ensure that the task we're running is the task we're supposed to kill. This isn't strictly necessary for our one-task executor, but it protects us from programming errors in the scheduler, in which we send kill messages to the wrong executor.

❹ We kill the process.

❺ We inform Mesos that the task was killed as per the user's request. Note the possible race condition if the thread crashes after calling `destroy()` but before sending the status update: Mesos might believe the task is still running. This is why we set `proc` to `null` afterward—it will ensure that a second kill message from the scheduler will cause the `TASK_KILLED` message to be resent.

We have now seen the entirety of how to implement a basic executor with functionality similar to the `CommandExecutor`. Of course, you might be wondering how to actually use this executor from your scheduler. To integrate this executor with our example scheduler from Chapter 4, we'll simply need to update the `makeTask` method of the `Job` object, as shown in Example 5-10.

Example 5-10. Enhanced makeTask for our new executor

```
public TaskInfo makeTask(SlaveID targetSlave, FrameworkID fid) {
    TaskID id = TaskID.newBuilder()
        .setValue(this.id)
        .build();
    ExecutorID eid = ExecutorID.newBuilder() ❶
        .setValue(this.id)
        .build();
    CommandInfo ci = CommandInfo.newBuilder()
        .setValue("java -jar /path/to/custom/executor.jar") ❷
        .build();
    ExecutorInfo executor = ExecutorInfo.newBuilder() ❸
        .setExecutorId(eid)
        .setFrameworkId(fid)
        .setCommand(ci)
        .build();
    JSONObject cfg = new JSONObject();
    try {
        cfg.put("cmd", this.command);
        return TaskInfo.newBuilder()
            // ... Elided unchanged code ... ❹
            .setExecutor(executor) ❺
            .setData(ByteString.copyFrom(cfg.toString().getBytes("UTF-8"))) ❻
            .build();
    } catch (Exception e) {
        e.printStackTrace();
        throw new RuntimeException();
    }
}
```

❶ We need to explicitly assign our executor an ID. The `CommandExecutor` uses the same ID for the task and executor, so we'll do that too.

❷ You'll need to build the custom executor's *.jar* and distribute it to your slaves. In the next section, we'll look at some approaches to this.

❸ The `ExecutorInfo` requires several pieces of information, including the `FrameworkID`. The scheduler was trivially modified to pass it to `makeTask`.

❹ The unchanged configuration to the `TaskInfo` is not repeated here (refer back to Example 4-3). We did, however, drop the `.setCommand(...)`, since now we're setting the executor.

⑤ `TaskInfo` must have exactly one of the command or executor set, but never both —that's an error.

⑥ Finally, we include the JSON configuration of the task.

That's all there is to it! Now we've enhanced our scheduler from Chapter 4 to support our new, custom executor.

Bootstrapping Executor Installation

One challenge in creating your own executor is deploying the binaries everywhere. We'll look at four solutions to this problem, and weigh their pros and cons:

Use HDFS, S3, or another non-POSIX store
Any Mesos executor can list a set of URIs that will be downloaded and optionally unzipped into the local working directory before the executor is launched. Mesos has built-in support for HTTP, FTP, and HDFS stores to download files (see "Configuring the process's environment" on page 94). As a result, you can easily host your applications on a local HDFS cluster, Amazon S3, or another data store to avoid the need to deploy any new technologies, as the other strategies might require. The challenge is that this data store must be sufficiently scalable to be able to deliver the container to every concurrently launching task. A common reason that a newly developed framework falls over during scalability testing is that it launches hundreds of executors simultaneously; these executors all simultaneously request their binaries from a single server, which kills the server. This is commonly known as the thundering herd problem (*http://bit.ly/thundering herdwiki*). Make sure that you sufficiently replicate the server that offers the binaries, or use a system with proven scalability, like S3.

The "next-level" version of this approach is to actually host the binaries in the scheduler process itself, by having the scheduler run an embedded HTTP server. Of course, this will exacerbate the thundering herd problem. The solution is to have the scheduler stagger the launch times of tasks, to ensure that the server is never overwhelmed. This is done by waiting for a random duration before submitting the launch to Mesos.

Use a configuration management system
Many Mesos clusters will be deployed using a configuration management system like Chef, Puppet, or Ansible. If this applies to your cluster, then you can also use that system to push your executor binaries out to every slave in your Mesos cluster. The benefit to this is that you can ensure that the binaries are always immediately available to launch tasks—you don't need to wait for them to download or run the risk of an untimely network failure that causes your tasks to become LOST. The downside, however, is that deploying and upgrading to a new version

of the executor is more difficult. Of course, you'll want to version every deployed executor (to ensure that multiple versions can be running concurrently, during upgrades); nevertheless, it can be extremely tedious during development to wait for the executor to be pushed out to all slaves.

Use a shared POSIX filesystem

Often, a compute cluster already has a shared POSIX-compatible filesystem. Some popular choices here are NFS (*http://bit.ly/NFSwiki*) and GlusterFS (*http://www.gluster.org/*). The shared filesystem approach is similar to the configuration management approach: in both cases, your executor exists at a known path. The benefit of having that path be on a shared filesystem is that you don't need to wait for the configuration management system to actually push the binaries out to every slave; instead, you can immediately launch the executor as soon as it has been copied onto the shared filesystem. The downside is that it can be difficult to scale the shared filesystem, and if it fails, your entire cluster goes down.

Use Docker

Mesos has first-class support for Docker containers (see "Using Docker" on page 129), which are themselves a way to ship around complete binary images. Once you Dockerize your executor, you can start that container on any slave in the cluster. The challenge here is the Docker repository: you must find a Docker repository (be it Docker Hub (*https://hub.docker.com/*) or a self-hosted one) that can host your Docker containers with sufficient scalability and security. The most common pitfall with this approach is the time to download a Docker container: when a Docker container takes 10 minutes to download, the executor launch might time out. This has the symptom of unpredictable, transient LOST tasks.

Now that we've reviewed several options, how do you choose the right one? If you are already heavily using Docker, then I recommend continuing with Docker to host your Mesos executors. Otherwise, if you have a shared POSIX filesystem, that option offers the fastest and easiest development. If you would rather avoid the challenge of setting up a shared POSIX filesystem for this purpose, then serving the binaries from HDFS or S3 still offers rapid deployment, and nearly everyone has this capability. Using a configuration management system does centralize deployment, but it dramatically slows down your ability to redeploy a newer or older version of an executor, and so it is an option of last resort.

Fetcher Cache

In Mesos 0.23, a new feature called the *fetcher cache* was released. The fetcher cache seeks to reduce the load on S3, HDFS, or other filesystems by caching executor downloads on every slave, so that they're downloaded only once per slave. Although this doesn't eliminate the scalability challenges with shared filesystems, it should help a lot. To fully take advantage of the fetcher cache and improve scalability, ensure that your scheduler staggers the launch of executors. That way, there will never be too many simultaneous requests to the shared filesystem, and the fetcher cache will further reduce the load. The fetcher cache guarantees that each artifact will be fetched once per slave; even if multiple executors request an artifact, they'll all wait for the single download.

To use the fetcher cache, you simply set `cache` to `true` in your URI protobuf in the `TaskInfo`. The fetcher cache is isolated by user, since it simply uses the URI as the key. In the future, there will be a way to bypass or purge the cache, but in the meantime, each URI should be unique for each different version of the resource's content.

In any case, remember that your scheduler specifies exactly from where and how to fetch and launch the executor. Consequently, each version of a scheduler can choose to launch different forwards- and/or backwards-compatible versions of the executor. By ensuring that your scheduler always launches a compatible executor, you can generally avoid internal version mismatches in your frameworks.

Adding Heartbeats

One of the advantages of the Mesos architecture is that temporary communication disruptions don't affect the operation of the running executors. We often leverage this functionality when designing for high availability, since each executor can continue to process its work or service client requests in spite of other failures. When building a pool of servers scheduler, for example (see "Pool of Servers Scheduler" on page 60), this is exactly the behavior we want. On the other hand, sometimes we want to ensure that every executor is running so that we can react quickly to failures—after all, there's no way to distinguish a temporary and permanent network blip.[2]

We'll ensure that every executor is functioning by requiring them to heartbeat every so often (the period will depend on how quickly we want to react to failures). To

---

[2] This is known as the FLP impossibility result (*http://the-paper-trail.org/blog/a-brief-tour-of-flp-impossibility/*).

heartbeat, we'll use framework messages, which have several interesting features and caveats:

- Framework messages are unreliable: there's no guarantee they're ever delivered.

- Framework messages are scalable: they usually use an optimized transmission mechanism directly from the executor to the scheduler, thus avoiding bottlenecking at the master.

- Framework messages can carry an arbitrary binary payload: you can serialize any data you'd like into them, such as progress updates.

- Framework messages are between executors and schedulers: it's up to you to include the task ID in the binary payload if you want to send messages about a particular task on an executor.

First, let's add heartbeats to our executor, as shown in Example 5-11.

Example 5-11. Heartbeats on the executor

```
public static void main(String ... args) {
    // ... snip ...
    Timer timer = new Timer(); ❶
    timer.schedule(new TimerTask() {
        public void run() {
            driver.sendFrameworkMessage(new byte[1]); ❷
        }
    }, 0, 5000); ❸
    // ... snip ...
}
```

❶ We create a new `Timer` when our executor starts up to manage the heartbeats.

❷ The task we create will simply send a framework message without any interesting data. In a production framework, you could include useful information here, such as when the message was sent (to track the message delivery delay) or what the completion percentage of each of the executor's tasks is.

❸ We start this task immediately, sending a heartbeat every 5 seconds. To increase scalability, heartbeats are often sent every 30 seconds or every few minutes.

Although it's easy to send heartbeats on the executor, we also need to augment the scheduler. First, we enhance the `Job` to automatically fail itself when it doesn't receive a heartbeat in time, as seen in Example 5-12.

Example 5-12. Automatically self-destructing Job

```java
public class Job {
    private Timer timer = new Timer(); ❶
    private TimerTask missedHeartbeatTask; ❷
    // ... snip ...

    public void heartbeat() { ❸
        if (missedHeartbeatTask != null) { ❹
            missedHeartbeatTask.cancel();
        }
        missedHeartbeatTask = new HeartbeatTask();
        timer.schedule(missedHeartbeatTask, 20000); ❺
    }

    public static Job fromJSON(JSONObject obj) {
        Job job = new Job();
        // ... snip ...
        job.heartbeat(); ❻
        return job;
    }

    public void succeed() {
        // ... snip ...
        missedHeartbeatTask.cancel(); ❼
    }

    public void fail() {
        // ... snip ...
        missedHeartbeatTask.cancel();
    }

    private class HeartbeatTask extends TimerTask { ❽
        public void run() {
            System.out.println("Heartbeat missed; failing");
            fail(); ❾
        }
    }
}
```

❶ Each Job will now have a Timer to manage the expiration of its latest heartbeat.

❷ We must store the TimerTask that will cause the current instance of the Job to fail, so that we can cancel it when we receive a heartbeat.

❸ The heartbeat() method will get called every time we receive a heartbeat from the executor.

❹ Every time we receive a heartbeat, we must cancel the current task, since if that task ran we'd fail the Job.

❺ When we receive the heartbeat, we schedule the next failure due to lack of heartbeat in 20 seconds. Since we expect a heartbeat every 5 seconds, this should only run if we miss several heartbeats in a row.

❻ When we first create the Job, we heartbeat it once to ensure that it fails if the executor never starts running.

❼ When the task finishes, we cancel the pending failure task, since it's no longer relevant.

❽ A HeartbeatTask is a subclass of TimerTask. We only need to implement the run() method, which is only called if the task isn't canceled before its time is up.

❾ If our task does get to run, we just fail() the Job, which will cause the Job to get rescheduled later.

Now that our Job has been enhanced to track heartbeats, all we need to do is pass along framework messages from the scheduler to the proper Job. To do this, we'll implement the frameworkMessage callback in the scheduler, as shown in Example 5-13.

Example 5-13. Implementing frameworkMessage for heartbeats

```java
public void frameworkMessage(SchedulerDriver driver, ExecutorID executorId,
                             SlaveID slaveId, byte[] data) {
    String id = executorId.getValue(); ❶
    synchronized (jobs) {
        for (Job j : jobs) { ❷
            if (j.getId().equals(id)) {
                j.heartbeat(); ❸
            }
        }
    }
}
```

❶ For the example executor in this chapter (and for the CommandExecutor), we set the executor ID to be equal to the job ID and the task ID.

❷ Since we don't care about the data in the framework message, we simply scan through all the current jobs to find if one of them has the same ID as the executor that just sent the heartbeat.

❸ Once we find a match, we call the heartbeat() method on that Job, so that the Example 5-12 code can do its thing.

This is all it takes to add basic heartbeating functionality to your framework. Of course, there are several enhancements that should be made in a production-quality system. Firstly, the heartbeat mechanism shown here creates one timer for every Job's heartbeat; for a system with hundreds of Jobs, every Job can share the same Timer to ensure scalability since each Timer creates a new thread. Secondly, this heartbeat system doesn't actually kill the non-heartbeating Jobs; it just treats them as dead. We should always kill the executors that aren't heartbeating by using the killTask API, or else we could end up with orphaned or zombie executors, which will consume resources indefinitely on the cluster without doing any useful work. Finally, when we're not sure if an executor was properly killed, we should be careful not to start an executor with a duplicate ID on a slave. We should actually track all the executor IDs we've used, and generate a new, unique ID for each executor. With the preceding code, you can encounter undefined behavior when you try to relaunch a Job on the same slave when the earlier executor is still running but believed dead due to lack of heartbeats.

Now, we've seen how to build a simple executor by leveraging the task-level and executor-level APIs. We've even added an additional functionality, heartbeats, that wasn't possible with the built-in executor. In the next few sections, we'll look at other advanced features that we can add to our executors.

Advanced Executor Features

As you've probably discovered by now, it's difficult to write an executor. Unlike most software that we write, the executor is particularly challenging to test, since we need to build it, package it, and ship it across our cluster, at which point we must wait to see whether it correctly interacts with our scheduler.

Before we start looking at additional features we can add to our executor, keep in mind that an executor doesn't have to make its task a subprocess. In fact, it's quite common to have tasks run in the same process as the executor—this can lead to greater efficiency and a simpler design. The only reason we split our executor and task into different processes was simply so that we could imitate the behavior of the built-in CommandExecutor in Mesos.

Progress Reporting

In "Adding Heartbeats" on page 113, we briefly touched on the idea that, in addition to using periodic framework messages to detect whether an executor is still running and accessible, we could include periodic status updates in those messages. However, we don't only have to use framework messages for this: the TaskStatus message also has a data field, and it too can be used to send updates about a task. Furthermore, it is possible to send multiple TaskStatus updates for the same status (i.e.,

TASK_RUNNING, TASK_STARTING, etc.) but with different values in the data field to reliably send a task's internal status changes. For instance, we may want to have our tasks report that they're RUNNING with the data value "initializing" when they start to initialize themselves, and then send a new status update that they're RUNNING with the data value "ready" when they're ready to begin processing requests. Let's look at the reasons we might consider to choose whether to communicate progress updates with status messages or framework updates.

Framework messages are highly scalable, because they are transmitted directly from the executors to the scheduler. Since the Mesos master typically doesn't process or forward framework messages,[3] the throughput of these messages is limited by the scheduler's ability to consume them. Furthermore, since framework messages aren't guaranteed to be reliable, during periods of high load, Mesos can choose to drop some messages in order ensure that higher-priority messages can proceed. These features make framework messages a great choice when scalability is the primary concern.

Of course, that scalability comes at a price: as mentioned, sometimes framework messages get dropped. Status updates, on the other hand, are guaranteed to be delivered. But this guarantee comes at a steep performance cost: every status update must be checkpointed to disk on the slave before it's sent, and then a second disk write must take place to mark the update as having been successfully sent. Furthermore, the slaves must keep track of all outstanding status updates, so that if a scheduler is temporarily offline when the status update would have been delivered, the slave can retransmit it later. This checkpointing and tracking, along with the periodic retransmissions of unacknowledged status updates, gives status updates their reliability, making them suitable for notifying the scheduler of important lifecycle events in tasks, at the cost of far greater resource usage and susceptibility to bottlenecks at the master's and the slave's disks.

Thus, the main criterion for whether framework messages or status updates are more suitable is whether every update completely subsumes all earlier updates. For example, if the goal was to report on the percent completed of a task, then missing the 49% update is irrelevant once the 50% update has been received (since the 50% update implies that 49% has already passed). For this purpose, framework messages are a good choice. On the other hand, if a task is reporting when various subtasks have been completed, each update is unique and they all should be delivered to the scheduler. For this purpose, status updates are more appropriate.

---

3 Technically, the Mesos master will sometimes process framework messages. This can lead to a bottleneck in rare cases, but the optimized bypass of the master is almost always used.

Adding Remote Logging

One often-encountered problem in building distributed systems is figuring out *"What the hell happened?"* This is so challenging because logs tend to be scattered across the cluster; this makes searching the logs for an error message much harder, since now we also need to search the cluster for the log. Furthermore, we often need to correlate several logs to identify how the interaction between multiple programs in our cluster resulted in failure. The most common way to mitigate this issue is to send all logs to a central repository, which then assists us in analyzing, searching, and correlating these logs. Some popular technologies for doing this are Splunk (*http://www.splunk.com/*), Logstash (*https://www.elastic.co/products/logstash*), and Papertrail (*https://papertrailapp.com/*).[4]

Recall how we used `ProcessBuilder.redirectOutput()` to send the `stdout` and `stderr` of our process to a file—we could instead get the `InputStreams` directly from the resultant process so that we can send the outputs anywhere. Once you're writing your own executor, you have complete control over where your executor's logs get sent, and where your tasks' logs get sent. For many applications, since there's only one task per executor, we want to send the executor and task logs to the same place. For other applications, however, we can actually send the task and executor logs to different places. This is useful when you want to be able to debug tasks separately from one another, and don't want to see all of an executor's tasks' logs intermingled.

Multiple Tasks

Mesos executors are designed to run multiple tasks. To run a task on an existing executor, you can launch that task the same as normal, except that you'll use an identical `ExecutorInfo` as the executor that's already running on that slave. To help you reuse executors, every offer has a field called `executor_ids`, which contains all of the `ExecutorID`s of the executors currently running on that slave; however, it's still up to you to store all the `ExecutorInfo`s and include them in your task descriptors. The master will validate the `TaskInfo`, so if you provide an `ExecutorInfo` that doesn't match the executor you want to launch on, the task will fail immediately with a `TASK_ERROR`.

---

4 You can read a summary and comparison of centralized logging solutions at Jason Wilder's blog (*http://bit.ly/centralizedlogging*).

Resizing Containers

A powerful feature of executors is that their size is always the sum of all the tasks they're running and the executor's resources. A custom executor is the only way to easily dynamically resize containers depending on what work they're performing. Of course, there's no free lunch: you'll need to keep track of which slave each executor is running on, and you'll need to use an offer from the existing executor's slave when you want to scale its container up.

Executors with expensive state

Typically, reusing executors is done when the executor contains some sort of expensive-to-construct state. For instance, the executors can be maintaining a local cache of a large amount of data that's stored in a slow external filesystem, like S3. In this case, the executor can be responsible for downloading that data, and then each task can access that data as a local file, which will be much faster than reading it over the network. Of course, there's always a trade-off: if you run multiple tasks at the same time on that executor, those tasks will run in the same container—you'll be giving up the strong isolation guarantee between tasks that Mesos usually provides! If you are confident that the tasks won't accidentally consume more of the container's resources than they should, this is a workable solution. If, however, you're like most developers and occasionally write bugs, this is a risky proposition, in that it opens up your framework to unanticipated interference and potential nondeterminism.

Multistage initialization

A less common situation in which multiple tasks are used on the same executor is when the executor has a complex initialization process. Rather than sending status updates as the initialization occurs, as suggested in "Progress Reporting" on page 117, the scheduler can treat each step of the initialization as a separate task. This way, the initialization logic can be managed on the scheduler, rather than on the executor. Although you'll occasionally see this technique used, I recommend against it. It is easier to implement the initialization state machine in the executor itself. This has the additional benefits of removing the need to implement parts of the state machine in the executor and other parts in the scheduler, and it reduces the dependency of the framework on a reliable network during executor initialization.

Canary tasks

There is, however, one situation in which an additional task on the executor is absolutely necessary: when we need to receive prompt notification that an executor that may not be presently running any tasks (but is waiting for new ones) has shut down or crashed. As mentioned in our discussion of `Scheduler` callbacks (see Example 4-6), the callback you might think would tell you when an executor is lost is never actually called. Therefore, to detect when an executor disappears, we instead run a canary task on it. That way, when an executor shuts down or crashes or its slave deactivates, we'll receive a TASK_LOST from the canary task, which tells us that the executor is lost. Of course, if you don't need to promptly detect that the executor has been lost, you could always just assume executors are gone if you don't see an offer from them within some timeout.

When should we use them?

The capability for executors to launch multiple tasks is a lesser-used feature, for good reason. The APIs can be challenging to use, due to the need to store the ExecutorInfos for reuse. Ultimately, multiple tasks should only be used in the following situations:

- When it's necessary to dynamically change the amount of resources used by an executor as its workload varies
- When the executor's state is so expensive to construct that it's acceptable to throw away the Mesos isolation functionality to save on reinitialization costs
- When the failure of an executor that might not be running any tasks must be detected rapidly

Use this feature carefully, as it can make debugging very difficult.

Summary

Executors are the Mesos abstraction for a framework's workers. They should be used when a framework requires richer interaction between its scheduler and workers. Building an executor is usually very challenging, because of the need to frequently deploy new builds to the cluster during development. By surmounting these challenges, you can build custom executors to enable frameworks to dynamically scale the containers in which their tasks are running, to efficiently share expensive resources, and to provide an easy API to send messages between the scheduler and workers.

In this chapter, after reviewing some of the reasons one might build an executor, we implemented an executor that was mostly compatible with the built-in Mesos CommandExecutor and which we integrated with the job scheduler from Chapter 4. Then, we added heartbeats, which allowed us to more rapidly detect certain types of partial failures on the cluster, resulting in a better experience for the humans that must wait for their jobs to complete.

Finally, we looked at some advanced uses of custom executors: how to choose between framework messages and status updates, considerations when integrating with centralized distributed logging systems, and how and why to develop executors that support multiple tasks.

Now that we've looked across the entire spectrum of building applications on Mesos —utilizing existing frameworks, building application-specific schedulers, creating rich executors—we'll move on to more advanced topics, such as Mesos internals, Docker integration, and exotic, cutting-edge APIs.

CHAPTER 6

Advanced Topics in Mesos

Although you now know the ropes of building applications on Mesos, you've probably got even more questions than when you started:

- What is the internal architecture of Mesos?
- How does Mesos handle failures?
- How can I use Docker with Mesos?

In this chapter, we'll learn more about all these things, so that you can build even more sophisticated, reliable systems.

Libprocess and the Actor Model

At a high level, Mesos is a hybrid strongly consistent/eventually consistent system, based on the message passing actor model, written in C++.

The actor model is a paradigm for programming concurrent and distributed systems. In the actor model, the developer implements *processes* or *actors*, which are single-threaded modules of code that process messages one at a time. While processing a message, an actor can send messages to other actors or create new actors. Actors can only send messages to those whose process identifiers (PIDs) they know. When an actor spawns another actor, it learns the PID of the newly created actor. In order to get more PIDs, actors must send the PIDs to one another in messages.

The actor model framework that Mesos uses is called libprocess, and it was written by Ben Hindman at the same time he wrote Mesos.[1] Libprocess is a C++ API that pro-

---

1 It appeared as a component of the Lithe project (*http://lithe.eecs.berkeley.edu/*).

vides actor model semantics and uses HTTP to communicate. Since everything speaks HTTP, it's easy to interface with libprocess.

Libprocess messages are just protobufs over HTTP, and can benefit from the headers, content negotiation, and routing features therein. A libprocess process is identified by its PID, which is written as the hostname and the port of the actor.

Fun Fact

In order to support the asynchronous semantics that the actor model requires, libprocess uses a neat trick: it turns out that HTTP status code 202 means that the request has been accepted and is being asynchronously processed.

For most users of Mesos, you'll need to understand nothing about libprocess and actors. If, however, you are using advanced containerization techniques (like Docker bridged networking) or have multiple network interfaces, you may need to configure the LIBPROCESS_IP and LIBPROCESS_PORT environment variables for the Mesos masters and slaves. These environment variables allow you to control which network interface the masters, slaves, and other libprocess actors bind to, so that their messages can successfully reach each other.

The Consistency Model

Let's talk more about the consistency model of Mesos. Where does it lie on the CAP theorem?[2] What guarantees do we get, as users and developers of Mesos? The answer to this question isn't simple. For this section, we're going to look at a Mesos cluster with three masters, the registry feature enabled, and the slave checkpointing and recovery features enabled. Really, any feature related to reliability and persistence will be assumed to be enabled, since they form the basis of Mesos's robust consistency model.

Consider the block diagram of Mesos while a framework is running a task in Figure 6-1. There are four parts: the master, the slave, the framework's scheduler, and the framework's executor. There are three communication links: between the master and the scheduler, between the master and the slave, and between the slave and the executor. Let's analyze the failure modes of each of these in turn.

---

2 The CAP theorem is a theoretical result about the possible and impossible behaviors of distributed systems. You can read about it in "Brewer's Conjecture and the Feasibility of Consistent, Available, Partition-Tolerant Web Services," (*http://bit.ly/gilbert_lynch*) by Seth Gilbert and Nancy Lynch.

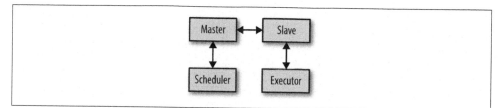

Figure 6-1. Message flows for a framework

How Is Slave Failure Handled?

First, let's look at the lifecycle of the slave, and see how various failures are handled. Initially, when a new slave starts up, it connects to Mesos and asks to register by sending a `Register` message to the master. The master then stores the slave's information in the registry, and once that operation has committed, it sends a `Registered` message to the slave, thus informing the slave that it's successfully joined the Mesos cluster. At this point, the master can begin to offer the slave's resources to the connected schedulers.

Suppose now that the slave crashes. In this case, the master will soon stop receiving the slave heartbeats, and after the configured timeout, the slave will be recognized as being "dead" and will be removed from the registry. As a consequence, even if the slave was only temporarily partitioned from the network, as soon as it resumes heartbeating or attempts to reconnect to the master, the master will politely inform the slave to kill itself.[3] At this point, let's hope that you're running your slave under a supervisor such as Supervisord, Monit, or SystemD. When the slave restarts, it'll generate a new random slave ID for itself, at which point it'll be able to successfully register as a new slave (see the following sidebar). When a slave crashes, any tasks that were running on the slave originally are LOST, since the slave is dead.

Fail-Stop Versus Fail-Recover

When academic researchers design new robust distributed algorithms, they typically work within one of two different models of the world: fail-stop or fail-recover. In the fail-stop model, whenever a machine crashes, it stays crashed forever; that machine never, ever returns to life. In the fail-recover model, machines that crash are allowed to return to life. As you can tell, the fail-recover model matches reality far more closely—after all, we fix and restart machines when they break; we don't just send them to the dumpster (or vendor) after their first problem! Unfortunately, it turns out that the fail-recover model makes it very hard to prove whether any algorithms

---

3 Note that if the slave reconnects within its configured timeout, the slave and all its tasks will continue as normal. This behavior is what zero-downtime live upgrades of Mesos rely on.

actually work, so much research is done within the fail-stop model. Interestingly, Mesos slaves emulate the fail-stop model with a clever trick—when you start a slave, its ID is not just the hostname of the machine it runs on; it is uniquely generated. This means that if a slave crashes and then restarts, it will get a new slave ID, and thus appear fresh to Mesos. This makes it much easier to reason about the behavior of Mesos. It's worth noting that the checkpointing feature of Mesos allows us, when we intend it, to let a restarted slave appear to be the old version. In this case, we treat the restart of the slave just like a brief network partition, rather than a crash.

How Is Master Failure Handled? (Or, the Registry)

Now, let's look at what happens if the master crashes. First and foremost, we know this isn't a big deal, as Mesos is built to handle all sorts of distributed failures. Plus, we've got those redundant backup masters around anyway, right? After the current master crashes, a new leading master is elected. Gradually the slaves will discover this information through the course of their regular communication with the masters. Since the slaves are heartbeating periodically, they'll see their heartbeats fail to connect or get rejected (depending on whether the old leader is down or merely restarted and now just a spare). The slaves will query ZooKeeper again to learn of the new master. At this point a slave will use a different RPC to connect to the new master, called Reregister, since the slave believes itself to already be registered but no longer connected. When the new leader receives this RPC, it checks the registry to confirm that this slave is indeed live. If it is, it accepts the slave's registration; however, if the slave was not in the registry, then it will tell the slave to kill itself so that it can be revived with a new slave ID and rejoin the cluster as a new slave without any baggage.

You might wonder why we need the registry and the reregistration process. Let's look at what happens if we remove reregistration and the registry. Reregistration's an easy one: if a slave can't reregister, then a master crash and subsequent failover will always force the slave to register as a new slave because (as discussed in the preceding sidebar) Mesos uses a fail-stop model. This means killing all the tasks on that slave. Needless to say, instantly killing all tasks across the entire cluster when the master needs to restart or fail over isn't ideal, and defeats the purpose of using a highly available cluster operating system.

Now, let's consider what happens if we remove the registry. Suppose that a slave stops heartbeating due to a network partition, and the old leader decides that slave is dead, meaning all tasks on it are considered LOST. Then, the masters fail over to a new leader, and at that time the slave, which was previously not sending heartbeats, miraculously manages to start sending heartbeats again. Now, the new leader will receive the slave's reregistration and accept it. But wait! The old leader thought that slave was dead, and sent the scheduler LOST messages about all of the tasks on that slave. Now we've gotten into an unfortunate situation where tasks in the LOST state seem to magically resurrect; this is a bug because LOST is a terminal state for the tasks. The registry allows us to ensure that tasks can never move out of the LOST state (or any terminal state) back into a nonterminal state: the old leader marks the slave dead in the registry so that the new leader will know to reject the reregistration.

One thing you might be thinking at this point is, "It sure seems like the masters will have to do a ton of bookkeeping to track what state every task on every slave is in, and store that in the registry." And you'd be right, except that the masters don't actually store any task information in the registry. Since the registry allows us to know which slaves are valid, Mesos allows those slaves to be the trusted, canonical sources of information about their tasks. So, when a master failover occurs, the new leader has no information about what tasks are running (and actually, the Mesos UI will reflect this, so don't be worried if it takes a couple of minutes after a master failure to see all your tasks again). Over time, as the slaves reregister and report in, the master will rebuild its in-memory picture of the state of the cluster.

There's one more consideration for the registry, however: *strict* and *nonstrict mode*. So far, I've only been describing the strict registry mode, since that's the safe, always correct logic. Unfortunately, there's an annoying limitation with the strict registry: you cannot add new slaves to the master until all slaves have either checked in or timed out (typically, there's a 90-second grace period for slaves to reregister with a newly elected master). If, however, you use the nonstrict registry, then your frameworks must deal with a very challenging case during reconciliation. In the next section, we'll learn about all the cases that can occur.

Reconciliation During Failover

At this point you're probably satisfied with the idea that Mesos will keep its state nice and consistent. Well, you shouldn't be, because there's still one problem as yet unexplored: how do the frameworks stay in sync with the Mesos cluster during transient failures? For instance, what happens if a master marks a slave as dead and then crashes, thus missing its chance to inform the schedulers about all the tasks on that slave that have just reached the LOST state (because their slave died)? After all, the leader's state about the tasks is 100% derived from the slaves' state, and the new leader has no idea what status updates have or haven't already been sent.

The answer to this dilemma lies in the reconciliation feature. Reconciliation is how a scheduler can check with the master to see whether the scheduler's belief about the state of the cluster matches the master's belief about the state of the cluster. A scheduler is allowed to, at any time, ask the master to reconcileTasks—this is an RPC that allows the scheduler to provide a list of all the tasks and their statuses to the master, and the master to provide corrections for any tasks for which it knows a newer status. Typically, reconciliation waits until the master is no longer waiting for slaves to check in (as would happen during a master failover); however, we'll see now how the non-strict mode of the registry complicates this.

Always Provide the Slave ID

Always provide the slave ID to the `reconcileTasks` RPC, even though it's optional. If you choose not to specify the slave ID, you may have to wait for up to two minutes for a response, since Mesos will wait until every registered slave has checked in or timed out. Also, you may erroneously receive a TASK_LOST message for some tasks, and later see those tasks resurrect. Rather than dealing with the excess latency and edge cases, just provide the slave ID for every reconciliation.

Task reconciliation can only provide details about a task when it's in a nonterminal state. Of course, the main reason to reconcile is to determine whether tasks are still running, or if they've moved to a terminal state. Whenever a task is in a terminal state, reconciliation for that task can always claim that it is LOST, when in fact it may have reached some other terminal status. It's the framework developer's responsibility to combine the information from reconciliation with other information, such as external services with which a successful task may have stored data, to determine what the true result of the completed task was.

Reconciling Completed Tasks

You should be careful to always ignore a TASK_LOST message from reconciliation when you've previously seen a different terminal status for that task.

As long as the task is not in a terminal state, reconciliation will result in the latest state for that task being sent (is either TASK_STAGING if the task hasn't sent any status update yet, or whatever the latest status update was). When the task is terminal, reconciliation is invalid. When the task's state is unknown to the master, however, the behavior is a bit trickier. There are a few situations to consider:

Task is unknown, but its slave is known
In this case, the reconciliation mechanism will report that the task has been LOST. This is logical because it means that the task has entered a terminal state.

Task is unknown, and the slave is in the registry but hasn't reregistered
This situation happens after a master failure before the slave has had a chance to check in. Mesos will simply wait to send a response to the request for reconciliation until it's heard from the slave, as it can't know what has happened to the task since the previous master crashed.

Task is unknown, and the slave is not in the registry

> If you follow the advice about always providing the slave ID to `reconcileTasks` and you are using the strict registry, you'll never have to deal with this confusing case. When this happens, Mesos can't know if it's ever going to hear from the slave, since that very slave may exist but not yet have been included in the registry. As a result, Mesos will report that the task is `LOST`, but you may see other status updates for that task if the slave registers later on. *This includes the chance that the task could appear to resurrect with a `RUNNING` status, or complete with a `FINISHED` or `FAILED` state!* Using the strict option for the registry completely prevents this case from ever occurring, and as such it is strongly recommended to run in strict mode.

Containerizers

As you know, Mesos has first-class support for Docker. But what does that mean? I mean, Docker can basically be run by a `docker run ...` on the command line, so what else needs to be done? Since Docker itself wants to manage the entire container, from the `chroot`, namespaces, and cgroups on through the entire userspace, it will conflict with the default Mesos containers. Because of this, Mesos has added support for *containerizers*, a pluggable mechanism to allow Mesos's containerization subsystem to be extensible: the original Mesos LXC/cgroups-based containers were ported to the containerizer API, Docker was added as the first new containerizer, and now there's a well-documented protocol for adding new containerizers, such as KVM virtual machines.

Using Docker

In order to use the Docker containerizer, you must include it on the Mesos slave's command line. For example, `mesos-slave --containerizers=docker,mesos ...` would allow Docker and plain Mesos containers on that slave.

You'll probably also want to increase the executor registration timeout, so that Mesos doesn't think that your container failed when it's actually still downloading. Five minutes is a good conservative starting point for ensuring that your Docker images have enough time to download. Thus, you'll end up with a slave command line like:

```
mesos-slave --containerizers=docker,mesos \
    --executor_registration_timeout=5mins ...
```

Using Docker with your application is very simple—once you've enabled support for Docker, you just need to set the `container` field (of type `ContainerInfo`) in the `TaskInfo` or `ExecutorInfo`.

Confusingly, the message `CommandInfo.ContainerInfo` is not the correct message—you want to set the top-level `ContainerInfo` in `mesos.proto` that has Docker-related fields.

To use Docker, set the `type` of the `ContainerInfo` to `DOCKER`, and set the docker field to an instance of the `ContainerInfo.Docker` message, which should have the `image` property set to your Docker image's name (e.g., `myusername/webapp`). At this point, you can configure many Docker parameters, such as whether to use `HOST` or `BRIDGE` networking, what port mappings to use, or additional Docker command-line options. If you'd like the Docker container to use the `docker run ...` specified in the Docker-file, then you should set the `CommandInfo` of the `TaskInfo` to have `shell = false`. If you set `shell = true`, then you'll disable the `run` built into the Dockerfile, and instead the specified `command` will be run via `sh -c "<command>"`.

When you launch a Docker containerized task, the slave first fetches (and unpacks) all the specified URIs into the sandbox, and it pulls the Docker image locally. Next, the slave launches the Docker image by running `docker`. The `docker` command's `HOME` environment variable is set to the sandbox, so that you can configure Docker via fetched URIs (as discussed in the following note). The sandbox will be available inside the Docker image, and its path will be stored in the `MESOS_SANDBOX` environ-ment variable as usual. Finally, Docker's `stdout` and `stderr` will be redirected to files named `stdout` and `stderr` in the Mesos sandbox.

Advanced Docker Configuration

One thing you should be aware of is that the Docker containerizer always attempts to pull the Docker image down from the registry. This means that you cannot use a local-only installed Docker image—you must have deployed it somewhere. If you'd like to use a private registry, you can provide a *.dockercfg* file. This file should be specified by a URI, so that the Mesos slave can use its automatic URL-fetching facilities to copy the *.dockercfg* into the `HOME` for the Docker process to use.

The same API works for Docker-based executors too, except that then your executor code can actually run inside the Docker container. To achieve this, do the exact same thing as described here, but in the `ExecutorInfo` message instead of the `TaskInfo` message.

The New Offer API

We've chosen to run Mesos because it allows us to flexibly allocate our workloads across our clusters, so that we can use our infrastructure more efficiently. Sometimes, however, we want to make longer-term allocation decisions with Mesos. For example, we may want to reserve certain machines to guarantee capacity for an application even when it's not running tasks. Of course, slave reservations exist (as discussed in "Static and Dynamic Slave Reservations" on page 18), but this new API allows us to make reservations programmatically, without shutting down a slave. We'll need a way to manage these dynamically created reservations on the cluster, which is where the new API comes in.

The launchTasks API that we first saw used in Example 4-5 has a drawback for some frameworks: once a task exits, whether normally or due to failure, its resources become available for other frameworks to claim. In this section, we'll take a look at the new offer API, which allows frameworks to dynamically reserve and release resources beyond the lifetimes of their tasks, as well as some of the additional features this API enables.

Framework Dynamic Reservations API

Dynamic reservations are a new feature that enables slave reservations to be made on the fly by frameworks that need to retain their resources through restarts (like databases and systems with strict SLAs). Rather than using the launchTasks API, we'll use the acceptOffers API. Example 6-1 illustrates two equivalent launchTasks and acceptOffers invocations.

Example 6-1. Comparing launchTasks and acceptOffers

```
driver.launchTasks(
    Collections.singletonList(offer.getId()),
    Collections.singletonList(taskInfo)
);

// Versus

Launch launch = Offer.Operation.Launch.newBuilder() ❶
                    .addTaskInfos(taskInfo)
                    .build();
Operation launchOp = Offer.Operation.newBuilder() ❷
                        .setType(Offer.Operation.Type.LAUNCH)
                        .setLaunch(launch)
                        .build();
```

```
driver.acceptOffers(
    Collections.singletonList(offer.getId()),
    Collections.singletonList(launchOp), ❸
    Filters.newBuilder().build() ❹
);
```

❶ First, we construct the actual command that we want to do with the offer—launching these tasks.

❷ Then, we construct the operation that we'll send to Mesos—all the different commands represented by the `Offer.Operation` union. Note that `Operation` is a protobuf tagged union (see "Understanding mesos.proto" on page 23).

❸ Here, we're only doing one operation on the offer. We could choose to specify a list of several operations, perhaps combining reserving resources, creating persistent volumes, and launching tasks into a single message.

❹ `acceptOffers` requires you to pass a `Filters` protobuf; feel free to just use the default, which does no filtering.

Besides using `acceptOffers` to launch a task, a framework can also reserve that task's resources as a dynamic reservation. When that task terminates, its resources are held in a reservation that's valid only for this framework's role. This means that you can launch your production workload, and in spite of it not having preconfigured static reservations, machine reboots and transient failures will not permanently disrupt its capacity (for services that must maintain a strict SLA) or functionality (for services that need to retain their data, like databases). Let's enhance our Java snippet to also reserve those resources. We'll add another `Offer.Operation` to the list of operations we are performing on those offers, as seen in Example 6-2.

Example 6-2. Reserving resources and launching a task in a single acceptOffers

```
Offer.Operation.Launch launch = Offer.Operation.Launch.newBuilder() ❶
                                    .addTaskInfos(taskInfo)
                                    .build();
Offer.Operation launchOp = Offer.Operation.newBuilder()
                                .setType(Offer.Operation.Type.LAUNCH)
                                .setLaunch(launch)
                                .build();

Offer.Operation.Reserve reserve = Offer.Operation.Reserve.newBuilder() ❷
                                    .addAllResources(taskInfo.getResourcesList())
                                    .build();
Offer.Operation reserveOp = Offer.Operation.newBuilder()
                                .setType(Offer.Operation.Type.RESERVE)
                                .setReserve(reserve)
                                .build();
```

```
driver.acceptOffers(
    Collections.singletonList(offer.getId()),
    Arrays.asList(reserveOp, launchOp), ❸
    Filters.newBuilder().build()
);
```

❶ As before, we construct the launch operation.

❷ We also need to construct the reserve operation; here, we're simply copying all the resources from the launched task so that the reservation for the task will persist beyond the task's lifetime.

❸ We can pass multiple operations into an acceptOffers. This is equivalent to waiting for the reservation to be acknowledged and reoffered by the master, but it saves a round-trip across the network.

Now that we know how to reserve resources and launch tasks on them, a logical question pops up: how do we determine whether an offered resource is from an existing dynamic reservation? Resources can have an additional field, reservation, that we can check to see if those resources been reserved, and by whom, as shown in Example 6-3.

Example 6-3. Querying resources for the reservation status

```
if (resource.hasReservation()) { ❶
    resource.getReservation().getPrincipal(); ❷
}
```

❶ This call will return true if the resource is reserved.

❷ If the resource was reserved, we can get the name of the principal that reserved it. The principal is often the same as the framework's user.

Handling Reservations in Offers

When using dynamic reservations, you may need to revise the code used to count how many resources are in an offer. Take another look at Example 4-10. Notice that we actually used += every time we encountered a CPU or memory resource. This ensures that we'll be able to use both reserved and unreserved resources for launching our tasks.

Once a slave dies, the reservation will be automatically freed. If your framework is tracking all the outstanding reservations, you can use the slaveLost callback to determine when a reservation on an old slave no longer exists. If you no longer need a reservation, you can free it by using the unreserve operation in `acceptOffers`, as demonstrated in Example 6-4.

Example 6-4. Unreserving resources

```
List<Resource> resources = new ArrayList<>();
for (Resource r : offer.getResourcesList()) { ❶
    if (r.hasReservation()) {
        resources.add(r);
    }
}
Offer.Operation.Unreserve unreserve = Offer.Operation.Unreserve.newBuilder()
                                .addAllResources(resources) ❷
                                .build();
Offer.Operation unreserveOp = Offer.Operation.newBuilder()
                            .setType(Offer.Operation.Type.UNRESERVE)
                            .setUnreserve(unreserve)
                            .build();

driver.acceptOffers(
    Collections.singletonList(offer.getId()),
    Collections.singletonList(unreserveOp),
    Filters.newBuilder().build()
);
```

❶ We find all the previously reserved resources.

❷ Here, we unreserve all of the resources that were previously reserved.

Reservations Are Forever

If you don't unreserve resources when you're finished, Mesos will continue to hold those resources aside forever, until you unreserve them. Dynamic reservations will leave beta once their administrative HTTP API is put into place. The HTTP API will allow the Mesos cluster's human operators to unreserve resources on a framework's behalf.

The dynamic reservations API is a powerful tool for building even more robust applications on Mesos. An HTTP API is available on the master as another way to manage dynamic reservations (see "Dynamic reservations" on page 19). This API makes it easy to alter reservations across the Mesos cluster on the fly. It also makes it easy to unreserve resources a framework may have left behind after it was shut down for the last time. Dynamic resources are just the start of the `acceptOffers` API; we'll now look at the persistent volumes API.

Persistent Volumes for Databases

Until recently, Mesos could only run services that didn't need to store data to disk. That's because there was no way to reserve the chunk of disk necessary. As of Mesos 0.23, reserving disks is now possible.

Remember from Chapter 1, you can think of Mesos as a deployment system. Wouldn't it be great if our MySQL databases automatically backed themselves up and created new read replicas as needed? Or if we could have simple, self-service REST APIs to create new Riak and Cassandra clusters? There's been work ongoing since 2014 to build database frameworks for Mesos. The issue with those frameworks is that every host has to have special data partitions created and managed outside of Mesos. With persistent volumes, projects like Apache Cotton (for MySQL) and the Cassandra and Riak Mesos frameworks will be able to independently bootstrap and maintain themselves.

In Mesos's design, disk space is ephemeral and isolated for every task. This is usually a good thing, unless you want to store data persistently. To solve this, Mesos introduced a new subtype of disk resources, called a *volume*. A volume is simply a chunk of disk that is allocated for a task and mounted at a specified location. The API for doing this is essentially the same as the Marathon API for mounting host volumes, see "Mounting host volumes" on page 41. You can even create a volume that isn't persistent, which will be useful in the future when multiple independent disks can be exposed to Mesos. Now, we'll look at how to create and use persistent volumes.

There are two `acceptOffers` Operations that are used to create and destroy persistent volumes. Unsurprisingly, they're called `Create` and `Destroy`. Persistent volumes can only be created on disk resources that have been reserved. Typically, you'll reserve the resources, create the volumes, and launch the tasks in a single `acceptOffers`, as shown in Example 6-2.

A persistent volume resource is the same as a regular disk resource (see "Resources" on page 13), but it has the field `disk` configured with the appropriate `DiskInfo`. The `DiskInfo` names the persistent volume so that it can be mounted by name via the nested string subfield `persistence.id`. The `Volume` of the `DiskInfo` should have the mode `RW` (as of Mesos 0.24, only `RW` is supported). The `container_path` field of the `Volume` will specify where the container will be mounted in the task's sandbox.

The persistent volume API is so new that no production frameworks have been written using it yet. It has limitations, such as that the volumes must always be mounted `RW`, and there's no way to expose multiple disks or have any disk or I/O isolation. The API will remain backward-compatible even as new features and functionality are added, though; because of this, projects such as Apache Cotton are already integrating persistent volumes into their codebases.

Summary

Mesos offers sophisticated, well-thought-out APIs for many different use cases. First, we discussed the internal architecture of Mesos at a high level, to help us understand why things are built the way they are. We then dove into a thorough analysis of how Mesos maintains internal and external consistency. By understanding the consistency model, we can build far more robust and failure-tolerant frameworks.

Next, we learned about the reconciliation process that is used to synchronize frameworks with the Mesos master. By understanding the mechanisms of the reconciliation process, it's possible to understand how to eventually guarantee consistency across a Mesos cluster, what types of inconsistencies can occur, and how to interpret those inconsistencies.

Then, we moved on to Mesos's integration with Docker, a popular application containerization and deployment format. By integrating containerization into frameworks, we can leverage broader ecosystems, such as all Dockerized applications.

Finally, we looked at dynamic reservations and persistent volumes, features enabled by the new `acceptOffers` API. Dynamic reservations allow us to far more easily guarantee capacity for critical workloads. Persistent volumes allow us to build database frameworks for Mesos that can persist their data in spite of unanticipated failures and faults throughout the system.

At this point, we've covered a variety of topics and techniques that are useful in building applications on Mesos today. In the next chapter, we're going to look at what's coming for Mesos tomorrow.

CHAPTER 7

The Future of Mesos

Mesos has come a long way. It started out as a graduate student project at the University of California, Berkley, but since then, it's been rolled out in production across hundreds of thousands of machines, attracting scores of developers to its ecosystem. We've learned about building applications on Mesos today, but where is Mesos going? In this chapter, we'll look at several current initiatives in the Mesos ecosystem that stand to become critical and valuable features of Mesos.

Multitenant Workloads

Before we discuss multitenancy, let's look at a motivating problem: noisy neighbors. Noisy neighbors are a problem in real life as well as in distributed systems with multiple users (tenants). When an apartment building's walls are too thin, you can hear your neighbors blaring music through the walls. Analogously, when a system doesn't provide sufficient isolation (i.e., thick walls), your application's performance can be adversely affected by other applications running on the same machine. For example, multiple CPU-intensive applications running on the same machine could all compete to use every CPU, resulting in reduced overall performance. As a result, it's hard for the users or cluster operators to predict the performance of their applications—whereas if those applications were running in containers, they'd each be guaranteed a share of the CPU, reducing the unpredictability of their performance.

Multitenancy refers to when a single resource (in our case, a Mesos cluster and the resources on its slaves) must be shared by many users, and the associated problems when those users accidentally monopolize what should be shared. You want a system that is designed for multitenancy, because it's much easier to have Mesos manage the isolation of resources rather than relying on users to carefully write cooperative applications.

Today, many Mesos installations benefit from containerization by isolating different applications from one another; in the future, more and more Mesos clusters will be isolating different users or customers from one another. Many large enterprises have struggled with multitenancy problems. For example, many companies administer and run separate Hadoop clusters for each team that needs a cluster. Why don't they just share one big cluster? Frequently, it's not possible for each team to achieve the level of service and performance they need if they can't predict how much the cluster will be utilized at any point. Separate clusters isolate the teams from one another, ensuring that each always can fully utilize the resources it needs. The separation of their systems is a solution to the noisy neighbor problem; however, since they're not sharing, the companies have to buy many more computers.

Mesos can serve multitenant workloads by allowing many users to share the same physical hardware (or VMs); with Mesos, Linux containers provide the isolation. Linux containers are a technology based on cgroups, open sourced by Google to enable high-performance isolation of multiple workloads on the same machine. Through projects like CoreOS, Docker, and Mesos, Linux containers have grown from an interesting but difficult to use technology into a powerful, popular, lightweight isolation mechanism. Although cgroups initially only provided support for isolating CPUs and memory, more and more Linux kernel subsystems are being integrated. For instance, in July 2014, Mesos added deep integration with the Linux network isolation stack. This allows for Mesos to be configured to control and isolate network bandwidth usage between containers running on the cluster. Currently, there is ongoing work to bring isolation to disk I/O usage between containers. Over time, we'll see Mesos get more and more isolation features added, which will continue to reduce the noisy neighbor problem in multitenant workloads.

There are also Mesos frameworks being built to solve multitenancy problems at a higher level, to make it easier for enterprises to achieve good isolation between different users of a shared Mesos cluster. For example, Myriad (*https://github.com/apache/incubator-myriad*) was started in 2014 by eBay to run YARN on Mesos. YARN is the resource manager for Hadoop 2.0. With Myriad, a single REST API request is all that's needed to create a new, fully isolated YARN cluster in Mesos. Thus, if you deploy Myriad, when a new team needs a Hadoop cluster for experimentation or production, there's nearly no administrative or operational cost. Another multitenant Mesos framework is Cook (*https://github.com/twosigma/cook*), written by the author of this book and open sourced by Two Sigma in 2015. Cook is a preemptive job scheduler; it's designed to allow any user to use as many resources as are available, but automatically scale that user back if other users' demand for capacity increases later.

Another way that Mesos supports multitenancy is through resource reservations. Reservations can be used to enable and enforce minimum quotas in multitenant environments, making them the strongest guarantee in a multitenant environment, at the cost of dynamic flexibility. If you believe that generally users won't monopolize the entire Mesos cluster, you can not bother with reservations and allow any framework to scale itself up or down freely. When some users have production-critical service-level agreements that must be met, you can use reservations to guarantee them specific resources. As of version 0.25, Mesos has added RESTful HTTP APIs so that cluster operators can easily create reservations for users on the fly, to simplify guaranteeing resources to particular users and workloads. There's also an initiative to add a RESTful quota API to Mesos, so that operators can allow Mesos to figure out reservations for them, based on high-level guidelines on how many resources each role should be limited to.

Mesos offers many features for building more robust multitenant systems. It integrates with the Linux kernel's resource isolation mechanisms to provide low-level isolation between tasks on the cluster. Framework authors are also aware of this problem, and more and more frameworks are coming out to simplify the management of multitenant clusters. Resource reservations are the most powerful tool for solving multitenancy problems: they absolutely guarantee a tenant resources, at the expense of preventing other users from accessing those resources. Now, what if there was a way for a resource to be reserved but still shared if it wasn't currently needed? In the next section, we'll look at the oversubscription feature Mesos added in version 0.23.

Oversubscription

What does it mean to utilize a cluster at 100%? To some, we're at 100% utilization when we have no more free resources on our Mesos cluster. However, even when a framework reserves a resource for a task (such as a web server), that task might not fully use all those resources. In fact, on most clusters, the actual usage is only 10–30%. To counter this, the Mesos oversubscription feature was created. It allows for Mesos clusters to automatically utilize their reserved but unused resources.[1]

To understand oversubscription, let's first define *slack*. Slack is the difference between what resources you think you're using and what you're actually using (Figure 7-1). Everyone's goal is to reduce slack: slack is just waste, where resources could be doing something productive, but instead sit idle. There are two kinds of slack on a Mesos cluster:

Allocation slack

Allocation slack is the difference between the resources available on the cluster and the resources that are reserved by frameworks. Mesos was engineered to address this type of slack efficiently, by repeatedly reoffering resources to all connected frameworks. This way, if one framework didn't want or couldn't make use

---

[1] The Mesos oversubscription feature is a solution to low actual utilizations, based on Google's Heracles (*http://bit.ly/googleheracles*) system.

of some resources, another framework could have the chance to use those resources. Some frameworks, such as Spark, take advantage of this by launching many small tasks that use few resources, so that they can get tiny allocations on many machines, driving cluster utilization up and exploiting those resources for their users.

Usage slack

Usage slack is the difference between the reserved resources and what resources are actually used. For instance, if a web server reserves two CPUs, it may be using nearly no resources if it's an off-peak time where it doesn't have many requests to process. The oversubscription feature is designed to allow Mesos to reduce this type of slack as well.

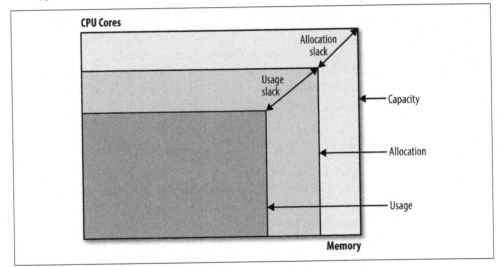

Figure 7-1. Allocation and usage slack of CPUs and memory

In some ways, Mesos has become a victim of its own success: allocation slack can be dramatically reduced on Mesos clusters, with commercial production clusters reporting allocation slacks of 5–15%, which is much lower than the 20–30% seen with earlier systems. So, a consortium of companies, including Twitter, Mesosphere, and Intel, set out to build a system that would enable Mesos to reduce usage slack. The result of their work is the Mesos oversubscription system, which applies control theory to usage slack on many resources.

To enable oversubscription, Mesos added a new type of resource offer: a *revocable* offer. Revocable offers are exactly like normal offers, except that tasks launched on revocable offers can be killed by Mesos at any time. By default, frameworks won't receive any revocable offers; they can opt in by adding the REVOCABLE_RESOURCES capability to their FrameworkInfos when they register. If the Mesos cluster has also been configured to enable the oversubscription mechanism, then any opted-in frame-works will see another type of offer along with normal offers: these special offers will have their `revocable` field populated, which means they can be canceled at any time. Note that currently an executor must have only revocable or normal resources; a mix of revocable and nonrevocable tasks cannot be launched on the same executor.

The oversubscription system is comprised of two pluggable components: the resource estimator, and the quality of service (QoS) controller. The resource estimator's job is to report to the slave how much slack is currently available in its running tasks, so that the slave can advertise the slack as additional resources. The QoS controller's job is to track the usage slack. When the usage slack decreases below what has been allo-cated to revocable resources, the QoS controller will begin to kill revocable tasks to ensure that the cluster's guaranteed reserved resources are provided.

In Mesos 0.23, there is only a single, fixed resource estimator, which allows a cluster administrator to have all slaves advertise fixed extra resources. This can be useful when you know that most tasks request one or two CPUs, but typically only use 5–10% of their resources. The fixed resource estimator can then allow every slave to have many more tasks scheduled on it than it actually has CPUs. Only a no-op QoS controller ships with Mesos 0.23.

Mesosphere and Intel are also building Serenity (*https://github.com/mesosphere/seren ity*), which is a sophisticated control system that repeatedly dynamically measures the usage slack on each slave, so that the cluster can utilize those resources. Serenity also understands how to estimate the impact of noisy neighbors, how to distinguish between a task that is starting up and a task that has reached its steady state, and other practical adjustments necessary to optimize cluster utilization.

Oversubscription is a powerful new feature that will help large clusters squeeze 10–40% more out of their resources. The revocable resources that oversubscription brings aren't only useful for allocating into slack resources; they will also form the basis of preemptable tasks.

Databases and Turnkey Infrastructure

Today, creating the complete infrastructure for an always-available distributed system is challenging. You need to set up databases, web servers, big data filesystems, analyt-ics tools, monitoring systems, and report generation processes. This is a lot of work—beside the challenge of sorting through the countless technologies and solutions in each space, every tool has its own specific way that it needs to be installed and config-ured. Creating a process to enable repeatable installation and configuration is often a major sticking point. On the one hand, one must typically write a large amount of bespoke deployment code to ensure that it's possible to reliably rebuild the entire infrastructure. On the other hand, it's very expensive and time-consuming to do so, and thus often that work will be deferred until the system has time to mature. Mesos stands in a position to change the way we approach deploying distributed application infrastructures.

Mesos has always been adept at running computation-oriented tasks, such as web servers and analytics frameworks. In version 0.23, Mesos finally added support for managing disks on the cluster. As a result, many data-oriented applications are now able to become Mesos frameworks. For instance, Cassandra (*https://github.com/meso sphere/cassandra-mesos*),[2] HDFS (*https://github.com/mesosphere/hdfs*),[3] and Kafka (*https://github.com/mesos/kafka*)[4] have already started seeing use on Mesos clusters. Over the course of early 2016, as the Mesos persistent disks API sees more uptake, Mesos's ecosystem will finally provide numerous robust choices for disk-based applications. One of the exciting projects to watch is Apache Cotton (*https://github.com/apache/incubator-cotton*) (formerly Mysos), which provides powerful automation for MySQL clusters.

In 2016, we're finally going to be able to simply install a Mesos cluster, and then ask the Mesos cluster to bootstrap our databases, monitoring systems, web servers, and analytics engines. This will dramatically simplify the amount of work needed to get a scalable, high-availability, self-healing cluster up and running. Since Mesos frameworks are running programs that can react to changing cluster conditions, they'll be able to automatically handle rote database maintenance and other standard cluster operation tasks. By automating these time-consuming tasks, operations staff will be able to spend more time focusing on other issues, such as application tuning and increasing utilization.

IP per Container

Another exciting feature coming for Mesos is IP per container. The problem we'd like to solve has two cases:

1. We'd like to use plain DNS names to have our browser automatically find tasks on our Mesos cluster (e.g., *mytask.mesos.mycompany.com*).

2. We'd like to more easily port applications that were built to run on an entire machine to Mesos (e.g., Cassandra, Riak, and other databases).

Mesos already has a DNS solution, called Mesos-DNS (*https://github.com/mesosphere/mesos-dns*). Mesos-DNS reads all the task metadata from the masters, and, for tasks

---

2 Cassandra is a high-performance NoSQL database, popular for its extremely high scalability.

3 HDFS, the Hadoop Filesystem, is one of the most popular big data filesystems.

4 Kafka is a high-performance, replicated queue that enables big data publish/subscribe workloads to scale.

that specify service discovery information or have alphanumeric-only names, Mesos-DNS will generate DNS records so that those tasks can be found through standard mechanisms. Alas, there remains a difficult problem: when a task needs to listen on some ports, most Mesos frameworks will dynamically allocate those ports based on what's available on the slave. As a result, even if you know the DNS name of the host, the browser will only try ports 80 (HTTP) and 443 (HTTPS). Thus, the browser won't be able to actually connect to the running application. Today, Mesos-DNS solves this by also serving SRV records, which include the port number that the service is running on. Unfortunately, browsers don't support SRV records, although you can use Nginx as a stopgap.[5]

The IP per container system solves this problem by allocating each executor its own specific IP address. This way, the DNS entry for the task points to the executor's IP address, and then the task can bind to whatever ports it wants on its private IP address. The way this works is that each executor's container gets its own Linux network namespace. This creates a separate network stack per container, so that the host can route traffic to the appropriate container. In addition, each network stack can have quality of service controls applied to it, so that each container can be assigned guaranteed network bandwidth. This feature will allow Mesos to manage IP addresses as first-class resources, like CPU, memory, and disk are today.

Summary

There are a lot of new and exciting features and plans in the Mesos ecosystem. Mesos has been built from the ground up to provide the strong isolation guarantees necessary to build out multitenant systems, and we've been starting to see that with systems like Myriad and Cook, as well as features like the network isolator.

Alongside the growing use in multitenant applications, Mesos is developing a sophisticated oversubscription feature that will enable the same type of high cluster utilization that Google has been able to achieve. This oversubscription feature as designed is easy to get started with (if you want fixed oversubscription), and advanced dynamically adaptive oversubscription is well underway.

Finally, persistent disks and IP per container are the last features needed to allow Mesos to offer the complete infrastructure management system that other products like OpenStack were built to serve. Mesos clusters can manage all of an organization's infrastructure, including analytics, databases, and services. Having an IP address per container will make it much easier to port legacy applications that require specific

---

5 Nginx can be configured to route incoming domain names based on SRV records with SRV Router (*https://github.com/vlipco/srv-router*).

port ranges, and to easily expose Mesos applications to end users without building complex routing and proxying layers.

Mesos is taking over the data center, bringing lightweight containerization, orchestration, and simple, centralized management to everyone with its open source ecosystem.

Index

HDFS, 5, 142
HDFS storage, 111
health checks, 43-45, 55
heartbeats/heartbeating, 100, 104, 113-117
HeartbeatTask, 116
Heroku/PaaS, 5
high availability, 79-85
host, 36
host information reporting, 11
host volumes, mounting, 41-43
HTTP Basic Authentication (HBA), 31
HTTP health checks, 44
Hubspot, 55

I

id, 33, 36
in-app discovery, 49
infrastructure improvements, 141-142
initialization, multistage, 120
instances, 33
Intel, 141
interval scheduling, 51
IP per container system, 142-143

J

Java keystore, 32
Java Virtual Machine (JVM), 98
job data, loading, 83-84
job implementation, 69-73
job processor scheduler, 62
job serialization, 84-85
job states, 76-79
jobs command, 1
jobs, automatically self-destructing, 114
JSON, 43, 53, 72, 101

K

Kafka, 26, 142
keystore (Java), 32
killTask, 109, 117
knapsack problem, 75

L

launchTasks, 68, 106, 131
leader election, 79-81
LeaderLatch, 80-81
LeaderSelector, 81
legacy applications, porting (see Marathon)

libprocess, 123-124
Linux containers, 138
logging, augmented, 100
Lost state, 127
Luigi, 54

M

make, 54
makeTask, 110
Marathon, 5, 29-57
    alternatives to, 55
    application versioning and rolling upgrades,
        45-46
    command-line options, 30
    event bus, 46
    HAProxy setup, 47-51
    health checks, 43-45
    placement constraints, 38-40
    placement operators
        CLUSTER, 39, 42
        GROUP_BY, 38
        LIKE, 39
        UNIQUE, 38, 43
        UNLIKE, 40
    REST API changes, 36
    running Chronos on, 52-54
    running Dockerized applications, 40-43
    running Mesos frameworks on, 51-55
        (see also Chronos)
    scaling, 38
    securing, 31-32
    setting up, 30-33
    specifying ports, 36
    using, 33-51
master UI, 9
master-executor communication, 11
MasterInfo, 67
masters, 8-10, 26
    and task metadata, 8
    failure of, 126-127
    for high availability, 9-10
    responsibilities of, 8-10
Mesos
    as a deployment system, 3-4
    as a DevOps tool, 3
    as an execution platform, 5
    benefits and uses, 6
    evolution of, 1-2
    internal architecture, 123-124

About the Author

David Greenberg works as lead architect at Two Sigma, where he oversees the distributed computation environment for the company's trading strategies. David's desire to learn has led him to study Russian and Chinese, and he enjoys practicing cooking techniques. He's also the designer of Cook (*https://github.com/twosigma/cook*), an open source Mesos framework for preemptive job scheduling.

Colophon

The animal on the cover of *Building Applications on Mesos* is the Indian giant squirrel (*Ratufa indica*), also known as the Malabar giant squirrel. Indian giant squirrels are arboreal, rarely leaving their treetop homes, and can be found living in forests throughout the Indian subcontinent. They play an important role in the forest ecosystem through seed dispersal.

The body of the Indian giant squirrel can grow up to 36 centimeters, and their tails can grow nearly twice as long. Their long tail provides balance, allowing Indian giant squirrels to move quickly from branch to branch. Their fur is distinctively colored, with dark brown backs contrasted against cream or beige heads, tails, and underbellies.

Indian giant squirrels generally live alone or in pairs. Their diet consists of fruit, flowers, nuts, tree bark, and insects. Their natural predators include big cats, birds of prey, and snakes. While Indian giant squirrels are not currently endangered, they are at risk of habitat loss caused by deforestation.

Many of the animals on O'Reilly covers are endangered; all of them are important to the world. To learn more about how you can help, go to *animals.oreilly.com*.

The cover fonts are URW Typewriter and Guardian Sans. The text font is Adobe Minion Pro; the heading font is Adobe Myriad Condensed; and the code font is Dalton Maag's Ubuntu Mono.

Have it your way.

Get even more for your money.

Join the O'Reilly Community, and register the O'Reilly books you own. It's free, and you'll get:

- $4.99 ebook upgrade offer
- 40% upgrade offer on O'Reilly print books
- Membership discounts on books and events
- Free lifetime updates to ebooks and videos
- Multiple ebook formats, DRM FREE
- Participation in the O'Reilly community
- Newsletters
- Account management
- 100% Satisfaction Guarantee

Signing up is easy:

1. Go to: oreilly.com/go/register
2. Create an O'Reilly login.
3. Provide your address.
4. Register your books.

Note: English-language books only

To order books online:
oreilly.com/store

For questions about products or an order:
orders@oreilly.com

To sign up to get topic-specific email announcements and/or news about upcoming books, conferences, special offers, and new technologies:
elists@oreilly.com

For technical questions about book content:
booktech@oreilly.com

To submit new book proposals to our editors:
proposals@oreilly.com

O'Reilly books are available in multiple DRM-free ebook formats. For more information:
oreilly.com/ebooks

CPSIA information can be obtained at www.ICGtesting.com
Printed in the USA
BVOW10s0555141215

430184BV00003B/4/P